Bigfoot Declassified

The Official Government Manual to Co-Existing with the Now Documented Species

M.P. RAYMOND

Illustrations by M.P. RAYMOND

iUniverse, Inc.
New York   Bloomington

iUniverse books may be ordered through booksellers or by contacting:

iUniverse
1663 Liberty Drive
Bloomington, IN 47403
www.iuniverse.com
1-800-Authors (1-800-288-4677)

ISBN: 978-1-4401-2218-7 (sc)
ISBN: 978-1-4401-2219-4 (ebook)

Library of Congress Control Number: 2009924017

Printed in the United States of America

iUniverse rev. date: Mar/12/2009:

CONTENTS

Section 3   63

INTRODUCTION

June 21, 20**

SYNDICATED NEW WORLD PRESS.......... "Most officials agree that the discovery of a Bigfoot creature on our country's soil could quite possibly create a series of very grave issues. If and when concrete evidence of the creature's existence is revealed, immediate problems will arise and our thinking will need to be radically modified. The word of this finding would spread around the world within hours; fear and panic would most certainly follow. Thousands of curiosity seekers, would-be hunters, and others wishing to capitalize on Bigfoot could create a substantial threat to public safety. There are some military officials who doubt whether any state or federal involvement short of dispatching the National Guard could keep order after a discovery of this magnitude.

The implementation of strict guidelines would be necessary for public security and well-being. A detailed program backed by scientists and supported by government security measures would be mandatory to guarantee the understanding and the control of these unique creatures."

CLASSIFICATION

Due to recent events, *Gigantopithecus karakus* has been added to the Official List of Known Living Species by the International Zoological Society (IZS). Chairman of the IZS and renowned paleontologist, Dr. Rupert Ainsworth, made this astounding announcement at the Society's recent bi-annual meeting. He indicated that the genus *Gigantopithecus* (including *G. blacki*, *G. bilaspurensis* and *G. giganteus*) has long been considered extinct. Yet, *karakus* seems to have branched off and managed to survive as a living viable species. For centuries, reports and sightings were thought to be fictitious, fabricated, and of isolated origin. However, these past events are now widely considered to have been authentic.

Newly reported information has surfaced and documentation has been acquired which indicates physical evidence to support and confirm the existence of the species. This evidence comes in the form of valid recorded information from various locations throughout the global community, and newly captured living creatures. These specimens have been studied via physical identification, DNA coding, and with a new universal classification method. At this time the validation of this species has been affirmed.

Gigantopithecus karakus -- most commonly known as **Bigfoot** -- has been entered as Classification #4762119 on March 31, 20**.

GOVERNMENT LIAISON

The government believes it would be beneficial to share a little something about the writer of the manual. We believe it will put the readers at ease and bring them into a comfortable state that will help move them through this mountain of interesting, astonishing, and potentially volatile material.

My name is Stuart Plainview. I live just outside of Washington, DC in the small community of Clearview Manor, VA. I have a lovely wife named Esther, and two children – David, 11 and Ruth, 9. My wife Esther is a wonderful homemaker, outstanding cook, and is well groomed. My children are your typical suburban kids, good students, both math team members and I just recently found out that David has been accepted into Chess Camp. I am so proud!

As far as activities of enjoyment, my wife and I go ballroom dancing at the Hall of Endearing Hope every Wednesday night at 7:30 p.m. We go to church every Sunday promptly at 10:45 a.m. and give generously when the collection plate is passed. We are also socially active in the community, volunteering for newspaper drives, flag pole dancing, Arbor Day events and other typical family activities. I guess you could call us average and maybe even slightly boring -- I'm not likely to disagree with you. I care about the things that everyone else does: safety for my family, job security, and good old-fashioned freedom.

A little bit about myself on an academic level; I have advanced degrees in both Dynamic Environmental Study and Macro Communications. I would have graduated at the top of my class if it wasn't for a severe bout of mononucleosis that kept me incapacitated for two months. My organizational skills are precise and methodical, yet I also possess a creative side, and once wrote a poem that almost got published. One odd little skill that I have acquired and honed over the years is that I can differentiate 17 different cheeses strictly by smell, which has come in handy on several occasions.

My typical work day starts by getting up at 5:38 a.m., having my cup of coffee and reading the Times while eating a small bowl of high fiber cereal with 2% milk. Esther makes me a lunch everyday that usually will include a ham and cheese sandwich, a hard boiled egg, yogurt, a piece of fruit, and a bottle of water or apple juice. This is all packed into a brown paper bag that I will use over and over for weeks. I am Eco friendly.

I leave the house every day at 7:14 a.m. so I will arrive at the office by 7:44 a.m. I park my 20** vehicle in the last parking space in the third row of the corporate parking lot. I enter by the south facing door which is opened by my electronic badge. I say "Good Morning" to Stanley the security guard as I step onto the elevator, which takes me up to the 11th floor where my office is located.

I work with a group of 20 people in a large office area that looks east over the Potomac River. I have a spacious office that has 3 large windows with beige Venetian blinds that shield the morning sun. There are several plants hanging in these windows that I tend to daily.

I have worked for the government for the past 15 years. I have had a variety of positions with various groups, the first position being secured right out of college. I currently work as a communications officer for the Federal Environmental Agency (FEA). I also chair the Environmental Security Edification Unit (ESEU), which I have been associated with for the last nine months.

It was on Monday, October 27, 20** at 11:15 a.m. that I was informed that I had been selected by our government to be a public liaison for an extremely sensitive matter. I alone will be in charge, and will be at the helm of the construction of a manual that will be issued to the American public. It will be a mandatory household reference guide pertaining directly to a specific topic: "*Gigantopithecus karakus*"-- more commonly known as Bigfoot.

I myself need to be more thoroughly educated and brought up to speed on the ever changing subject matter regarding this creature. In the past nine weeks, I have been debriefed by our top government officials and by leaders in numerous scientific fields. I have attended meetings in corporate offices, secret habitat facilities, secured government locations, coffee shops, discussion rooms in the Vatican, and even a strip club. (My wife was most disturbed by that particular meeting). I have had these meetings to gather the information needed for my work. My travels have taken me from North America to Europe, Russia to British Columbia, and from Asia back to Washington. The information to which I have been given clearance will be for the sole purpose of constructing this manual and it is nothing short of staggering.

In conjunction with the departments of security, intelligence, investigation, and the military, the FEA and I will issue this comprehensive manual that will provide information that the government feels the average citizen needs to know about Bigfoot. With this text you will gain knowledge that will prepare you and allow you to comprehend this recently recognized species. It will examine the most telling of encounters that predate the official discovery of the creature. You'll read the harrowing tales of unprepared people. You will learn what is being done at the present time to help educate and prepare you, as well as how to control these creatures. We will show you the findings we feel you need to know and why we have chosen now to teach this preparedness.

What was once only a myth is now our reality! The reality is that Bigfoot is with us now, and always has been. No longer are we dealing with grainy film footage or a blurry photograph, these are elements of the past. Unclassified film footage by dozens of witnesses and the increasing amount of sightings daily is the present norm. Now the average American wants to know how this will change his life. How will this phenomenon affect me, and how can I protect myself and my family from this creature? This is uncharted territory for all American citizens, and a discovery process for everyone involved.

Bigfoot has now been studied directly; we no longer need to surmise its true behavior. On some levels, this information may appear unorthodox in its delivery and structure, and not what the average citizen would expect to find in a government generated text. What is being addressed here is a very unusual subject matter, which in itself is directing the feel and flow of this sensitive material. The government has gone to great lengths to study the nature of Bigfoot and pass that knowledge on to the public so that we all may feel safe and secure.

SECTION I

Purpose for this Government Text
Historical Perspective
Recent Documented Stories

In light of new information regarding Bigfoot -- more sightings, newly recorded videos, close human interactions, and stories reported on the internet -- the government has found it necessary to publish a specific manual about this creature. No longer are they able to secure pertinent details and reports of encounters and events. There are too many occurrences that cannot be silenced. Due to the volume of recent activities, the government has no choice but to inform all citizens for security purposes. With that being said, this is the main reason I have been appointed to construct this document.

This manual will provide all the definitive answers that the average person will need to know to deal with any Bigfoot situation. This is a government-approved text and should be used as a reference for all questions related to Bigfoot encounters. This information has been delineated with the utmost scientific backing so the American public can feel secure in following our direction. We do not endorse, support, or approve of any other published material regarding this matter.

Reason for Concern / Education

Although amateur research and documentation of this creature's occurrences have been available for some time, the identity of Bigfoot in North America has been one of mystery until recently. Much speculation has arisen as to the reasons why Bigfoot has suddenly appeared out of the woods and into our lives at this time. Scientists have offered a myriad of explanations: climate changes, deforestation, wildfires, urban sprawl, and increasing population. Some less reliable sources have theorized that a number of other possibilities are potential causes. They tend to be more on the fantastic side, with Bigfoot being labeled as the Omen of Doom, the Grim Reaper, or even the Anti-Christ! These beliefs, however, are only fabrications of creative minds.

Extinct Species?

According to zoological history, this type of emergence has occurred before in a variety of species. Animals that were once thought to be extinct are found alive and well, living in secluded habitats not yet inhabited by humans. The Coelacanth, for example, is a fish that was thought to be extinct since the late Cretaceous period. In 1938, a fisherman off the coast of South Africa happened to catch one in his nets. A scholar friend of his was surprised at the unusual fish and went on to identify the find using not current identification methods, but fossil records.

On the other side of the ocean, in the dry shrub regions of South America, a relative of the domesticated pig can be found called the Chacoan Peccary. This little animal was also thought to be extinct and only identifiable through fossil remains.

However in 1975, it was found by scientists to be flourishing in parts of Paraguay. On a side note, the local population recognized the existence of the animal when science could not and said the best feature of this pig species is that it tasted like sweet ham. We must keep in mind that most eyewitness accounts are seldom used as scientific proof unless they can be substantiated by physical evidence.

There are also examples of species where there are no fossil records to go by and only fleeting eyewitness accounts of the subjects. In these cases the animals in question garner little scientific attention and the sightings are often ignored. Such are the cases of the Okapi and the Giant Squid. The Okapi of the African Congo were thought to be a myth by early Europeans who arrived on the continent. They originally thought it to be a type of jungle horse. Later, natives would lead the Europeans to bones and bits of hide, but there were still skeptics. It was not until 1902 that a live specimen was captured and discovered to be real. It is a close relative to the giraffe and has markings similar to a zebra. This fantastic description could be why accounts of the animal were dismissed.

The Giant Squid is another beast previously thought of as mythical, instilling fear into the hearts of many sea-faring men. Supposed sightings and questionable remains have always been presented but without having any real credibility. It wasn't until 2004 that an actual photograph was taken by a scientific expedition that proved the creature was real. It would be almost two years before a similar expedition was able to capture video footage of the squid feeding in the depths of the ocean. Still today, there is little knowledge of this water beast.

An additional story that should be discussed pertains to a popular "extinct" species called the Red Crested Button Bird. Named for the round, button-shaped red pattern on its throat, the Red Crested Button Bird is a type of finch that was discovered on an uninhabited island in the South Pacific in 1975. Scientists who had been staying on the island while studying the effects of red bloom in coral reefs first identified this species. During most late afternoon and early evenings at the campsite, they began to notice two strange-looking birds darting through the campsite at eye level. They found this odd because most birds on the island would fly above the campsite in the trees, and never with night closing in. These birds would fly through at no higher than six to eight feet above the ground.

The peaked interest of the researchers led them to contact a team of avian specialists, who upon arrival, intended to capture one of these odd birds in order to conduct simple observations pertaining to height dynamics of flight. Upon capture and subsequent testing, they determined the birds would not fly more than six feet above the ground, even when introduced to predatory stresses.

Eventually, a test was devised to examine their reaction to increased height. The birds were placed in a cage that was hoisted by a rope and pulley into the air. Strangely, as the bird was lifted above six feet high, its heart rate increased dramatically. This was exhibited by elevated levels of wing-flapping and chirping. If the bird was lifted above the six foot threshold and not lowered within a certain amount of time, its heart level was raised so high that it suffered a heart attack. The avian scientists concluded from these tests that the Red Crested Button Birds were afraid of heights. This may have been an evolutionary environmental influence, a result of living in a habitat with low height level shrub and tree growth. This habitat would offer protection and apparently there were no ground-level predators to impart pressure on their territory. There was also a high availability of food and water in the habitat in which they lived. The trees and shrubs flowered for the entire year and the nectar derived from the vegetation provided the majority of sustainable nourishment needed for survival.

In an effort to study these marvels of nature further, the team of avian scientists collected seven birds for transport to a research center in California. They were placed into small cages covered with dark cloth, and put aboard an airplane freighter. A porter heard the birds singing while he was loading them into the cargo area and thought that they should be near a window with views of the journey. He took the cloth off the cages, not knowing that this was for the birds' protection. The result was extreme stress to the birds, as the altitude of the freighter was significantly higher than six feet. All seven of the birds perished, having been scared to death of the height they perceived while restrained in their cages. Upon discovering the dead birds, the scientists decided to go back to the island and gather more specimens. They searched for weeks but were unable to procure a single specimen. In a matter of weeks, the newly-discovered species had vanished due to its interaction with man.

Using this knowledge of past unknown theorized species may help us to begin to understand what the discovery of Bigfoot really means. Is this a real being, another scary story, or just an unrecognized concept? This case is unlike that of the okapi and the giant squid, where no fossil evidence was found. We had solid proof that at one point in time, *Gigantopithecus* actually did exist, possibly going into deep hiding for extended periods of time. There's no question that humans have always told stories of wild men in the woods or giants of the earth. In the last 60 years, evidence has been collected but none of it has been conclusive. It took an undeniable video account of this beast, as well as the physical capture of a live specimen, to prove beyond the shadow of a doubt that it continues to exist to this day, however improbable that may seem. We must be ever vigilant in our study of this new species.

It has been theorized that *Gigantopithecus karakus* (Bigfoot) was not an antecedent of man, but a convergent species. This was an animal that was aware of man, possibly dealing with him on a regular basis. Following this concept, it can also be surmised as to why Bigfoot went into hiding. Did it compete with humans for food, water and habitat? It can be postulated that due to its size and/or relative appearance to man and his primeval behavior that the two species simply could not co-exist. Primitive man was likely frightened by Bigfoot, and it is possible that he tried to scare it off, and at times hunt Bigfoot for food. This ancient relationship is manifested in several modern encounters, usually described as occurring interests, but generally fearful for both species. The most likely scenario is that of humans intimidating the Bigfoot to the point where it had no choice but to retreat into hiding. What we have learned now of Bigfoot will most certainly alleviate any fears that we may have of the creature and hopefully allow us to coexist peacefully.

In comparison, man can also be an elusive species. In the modern world, there are still over 100 distinct native tribes worldwide that have had no contact with the outside world. Over half of these groups live in remote areas of South America. We are describing groups that upon seeing civilized man are extremely guarded and fearful. They have no concept of an integrated society, with its infrastructure and technology. Here are groups of human beings that still find a way to isolate themselves from contact with developed societies. Bigfoot is an animal with this same base instinct on its side, helping it to go unnoticed, at least until this point in time. When we assume that it should have been much easier to identify Bigfoot, we are fooling ourselves. We recall how difficult it was to identify tribes like the ones mentioned above. Bigfoot is an animal that did not wish to be discovered. It was operating on its instinct to stay in the hidden areas of the wild.

Now we must ponder the question: why has Bigfoot suddenly emerged? One of the most widely-held theories suggests the emergence is due to food needs. The most common reports from eyewitnesses are those of a Bigfoot disturbing trash receptacles or foraging through agricultural areas. It is suspected that certain habitat changes are forcing Bigfoot to expand its range of where it is looking for food. It is now going into areas that once would be considered rare. It is possibly aware of the potential dangers to which it will expose itself by going into these areas, but what choice does it have? It needs to eat, and in order to survive, it will come out of hiding to do so. What exactly is affecting its natural feeding sources is not altogether clear. It is thought to be a combination of a number of factors.

The most pronounced factor is widespread severe drought conditions that have been brought on by increased temperatures. Human deaths alone are increasing due to heat stroke. This may also be affecting animal life that is typically more sensitive to environmental conditions. Increased temperatures directly lead to amplified energy consumption and water usage. Already, major urban areas are strengthening water usage bans. Any water used by humans is being directly siphoned from rivers and reservoirs that are possible sources for Bigfoot.

In the last decade, we are seeing an increase of natural disasters across the board. The disasters most relevant to Bigfoot habitats are wildfires, which, especially in the last decade, have destroyed millions of acres and prevented a viable natural habitat for generations to come. This deforestation has been prevalent in the Pacific Northwest which, as we now know, is an area more heavily populated by Bigfoot.

The forests that have not been damaged by wildfires are now subject to another concern: the taking of land for profit and development. Man's development has also pushed Bigfoot out of its land and has pressed it to move deeper into the forests. This development has eaten up thousands of acres. Each day, Bigfoot's habitat shrinks.

Yet another of the major dangers threatening Bigfoot is man-made pathogens that invade its water supply. Climate changes and human development in natural areas are causing dangerous shifts in the ecological balance. Where there were once natural defenses, microbes and chemicals are now tearing down vegetation and wildlife. This has direct affect on Bigfoot's food supply and its total well being.

Historical Perspectives

The name Bigfoot stirs up the public sector and usually leads the collective thought in the wrong direction. The population, having perceived Bigfoot as a mythical creature, is now forced to look upon hard facts and valid documentation of its existence. Bigfoot, the largest of the great apes, has really only been a modern popular fascination since the mid-60s. However, if we look farther back in time, we will find that the cultural memory of Bigfoot has existed since the beginning of recorded history.

There is a school of thought that believes Bigfoot originated in prehistoric times. During the Pleistocene era there may have been a mighty giant man-ape creature roaming the plentiful forests of the great land mass called Pangaea dating back over 225 million years ago. Researchers believe that the creature inhabited portions of the supercontinent that would now be the present-day areas of Asia and North America. It was said to have thrived for hundreds of thousands of years, before succumbing to extinction.

Did this creature plummet into extinction, or did it just stay hidden away during man's territorial push? There are reports of its living in the great Johor National Park in Malaysia. This forest is vast in size, and is over 250 million years old. According to researchers, it would have been able to sustain a creature of the magnitude of a Bigfoot. There were plentiful resources, food, water, and enough space for such a creature to stay veiled in secrecy for centuries.

Ancient biblical text describes "Giants in the Earth" (Genesis, 6:4) -- creatures that walk like men but are not our kind. In 79 A.D., Pliny the Elder describes a large Himalayan creature that had a "human like body". This creature, known as the Yeti, has roamed from Tibet to Pakistan for centuries and is legend to many in that land. Native American lore describes a wild man in the woods and early explorers of North America were warned by the Native Americans of these large hairy men. In the 1800's the idea of Bigfoot was that it was a normal man gone "wild", thus the "wild" name descriptions.

Early evidence suggests that some Native American tribes had close ties to Bigfoot. These encounters were of peace, harmony and respect. These particular Native Americans honored these great creatures and looked upon them with a sense of awe and mystery.

A group of coastal Indians from British Columbia called the Kwakiutls featured carved forms of a large hairy beast on totem poles. This is one of the earliest references to Bigfoot ever recorded. Even on a spiritual level, the idea of a large bipedal primate runs deep in Native American history. Bigfoot was viewed as part-animal and part-man: a creature of the highest level.

Bigfoot was never considered just an animal, but was thought to be more along the lines of an elder brother or teacher by many Native tribes. Some of the tribes also believed Bigfoot to have power and ability to access a special place, which they considered sacred and part of an afterlife found only by supernatural process. Bigfoot was seen as one that would share its natural wisdom to all who would look, listen, and learn. This would happen not by voice, but by its appearance, its energy, its power, its very self. Bigfoot represented the coming of a new day, or a new world. With its power, spirit, and presence, it could move smoothly through the wooded world as if no tree, brush, or shrubbery existed. Bigfoot was said to exist in different dimensions. It would come into our world and let us be graced by its presence when it sensed an appropriate time to do so.

(Note: The government does not substantiate this Indian view and we find it most disruptive to our goals.)

Bigfoot Nomenclature

There have been numerous sightings of Bigfoot throughout the world, beyond, North America. Below is a list of names that have been used to label this great creature. These names may be different depending on what part of the world Bigfoot has been sighted, but all pertain to a very large and hairy biped that is thought to be half man, half ape.

Domestic and North American Names:

- o Sasquatch – Native American
- o Wildman of the Woods, Wild Child, Wild Boys -- various U.S. locales
- o Old Sheff -- origin unknown
- o Fouke Monster -- Fouke, Arkansas
- o Momo the Monster -- Missouri
- o Skunk Ape -- Florida
- o Old Yellow Top -- Canada

Other Global Names:

- o Almas -- Mongolia
- o Chuchuaa -- Siberia
- o Hibagon -- Japan
- o Kapre -- Philippines
- o Yeren -- China
- o Yeti -- Tibet
- o Yowie -- Australia

In the late 1800's, in the Willow Creek area of the Cascade Mountain, there were widespread reports that a man-like creature and its family roamed the place known as Bluff Creek. This is one of the earliest reports of a Bigfoot inhabiting an area so close to man. One creature was said to be 8 feet tall and over 700 pounds. They were all said to be lightly covered with hair, smelling foul, and prone to leaving footprints for miles. The sightings faded away and then returned in the early 1930's, when more footprints suddenly appeared. After a brief dormancy, sightings began again in the late 1950's, during the construction of logging roads. Evidence of heavy equipment being moved, tossed oil drums, tractor tires thrown about, substantial footprints, along with odious smells added to the legend which still lives today. This, combined with over 170 reliable sightings, has led the community to show respect to the mighty creature and its wonder by erecting a monument to the legend. Willow Creek today is regarded as the "Gateway to Bigfoot Country."

It wasn't until the 1960's that the public at large began to embrace the concept or idea that there was a real, breathing, previously uncategorized animal living in their midst. The most famous and biggest encounter occurred in 1967, when two amateur filmmakers exploring the woods of Bluff Creek, California filmed footage of a supposed female Bigfoot! This footage caused excitement and a revived interest in the pursuit of Bigfoot. This encounter was the evidence that many people were looking for. There were those who believed this to be too convenient, regardless of the respected names that backed the footage. Skeptics came out of the woodwork and simply could not believe what they were seeing.

Most accounts prior to the Bluff Creek encounter were recollected only from memory. They observed with their own eyes the gigantic size and breadth of this creature. Descriptions of the hair color (black, brown, or reddish), the length of its enormous arms and chest, and countless observations of footprints left behind have been (recorded/remembered) as part of history. These eyewitnesses also remembered the shape of the conical head and the flat, stout nose. People heard with their own ears the growling, grunting, whistling, and heavy breathing of this beast. Probably the most intense of all memories was the smell that exuded from Bigfoot. However, when people told their horror stories of seeing large creatures and sightings of human-like animals, most listeners would tend to think that they were either crazy or had been drinking too much. It was not until the 1967 film footage came out that these people received some validation that they might indeed be right about what they saw, heard, and smelled!

In most cases a Bigfoot encounter is very placid. The creature can generally be seen foraging in an unsecured wooded area. While historically displaying guarded behavior, Bigfoot seems to have become accustomed to humans and perceived them as a limited threat. They are generally drawn to interesting sounds and seem to have an affinity for certain types of music, while others will be driven away because of this. There are a number of cases where Bigfoot has been drawn in by the sounds of a television, coming from a great distance away. This sounds like a garbled whisper to Bigfoot, and it has been shown to soothe the creature.

Generally they don't enter the household, but have been found peering in windows, seemingly mesmerized by the television sounds, or by the variety of images floating on the screen. Bigfoot sightings have taken place in the deep woods or in rural populated areas that border wilderness. Eyewitness reports would include disturbed hunting cabins, molested campsites, or occasional glimpses of the mysterious creature crossing the road. However, this is no longer considered the norm. We are seeing a dynamic increase in sightings and encounters in more heavily populated suburban areas. There are even a few isolated cases where Bigfoot has wandered into the outskirts of the city areas that border heavy forests.

A great number of encounters with Bigfoot have been mostly by chance in secluded areas far away from civilizations. These encounters would be in areas that are part of what is considered the Bigfoot habitat range. This great range was similar to that which was traversed for many years by the Great Buffalo and Bison. This is analogous to the Bigfoot range, with the animals living in secluded areas, no man around, surviving on their own off the land. As soon as man entered their territory, sightings became more routine, more common, more likely.

Originally, the government would neither confirm nor deny that Bigfoot existed, and most inquiries were met with skepticism. The matters were documented and logged in a ledger, only to be filed away. What actually occurred behind the scenes was very different. The government was initially very alarmed at the prospect of a 7 to 9 foot creature invading our main streets. The social implications of government-developed rules and regulations, plus the costs associated with their enforcement would be staggering. The government had admitted to collecting and quantifying data found by amateur researchers of Bigfoot encounters, but could not justify any cost effectiveness in such a "far-fetched" matter.

Prior to this, each witness associated with any encounter was debriefed, and essentially misinformed about what they had seen, in an effort to contain the information. Witnesses were told that they had seen an escaped circus gorilla, a bear, or special effects for a movie production, and many accepted these explanations. There were some stubborn individuals who were adamant about their stories and refused to go along with any government protocol. It has now become evident that these events are far too widespread for effective containment. All the while, the government has maintained an appearance of disinterest in order to minimize the potential impact, and has required that a Bigfoot would need to be captured alive, in order to admit its scientific existence.

Bigfoot Sightings

2009

©2008 M.P. Raymond

Present Day

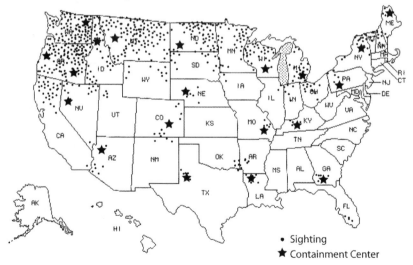

- • Sighting
- ★ Containment Center

The Country is Changing: Stories

There have been many stories of human interaction with Bigfoot, most as varied as the situations in which they occur, but sharing some common elements. For example, it has been typical in farming areas to receive reports of livestock being seized or disappearing without a trace or reason.

Millie Thompson of Cascade, Washington managed a small farm that included a moderately sized vegetable garden, one cow, four sheep, six pigs, and a henhouse containing about twenty chickens. She recalls that during late summer of 20**, for a short period of time there were some mysterious, odd occurrences happening on her farm. Someone or something was taking livestock, chickens, and vegetables from the garden. She also noticed extensive amounts of water being taken from the pigpen. She remembers waking up one morning to discover that one of her sheep had disappeared from her farm. The sheep had been penned up inside a good sized fenced area; there was no evidence of foul play, or damage to the fencing.

Later that same week, she noticed rows of corn had been disrupted and there were many missing vegetables in her garden. One commonality of these strange events were the large footprints noticed in the area where damage or loss had resulted. On another day when going out to feed the pigs, she noticed that all the water was gone from the troughs. Ms. Thompson was sure that the pigs did not drink all the water. She again noticed there were some very large footprints in and around the pig pen. This went on for about three weeks; then, just as quickly as it had started, it ended. She was never able to identify what or who was damaging her property. Upon telling her stories to local town officials, they all speculated that it was in fact a wandering Bigfoot.

Another example of a Bigfoot encounter with damaging results happened to a farmer in Oregon named Jed Buckley. He describes the story of how he had a henhouse with about 200 chickens, and how it had been raided one night. The chickens were raised mainly for egg production for local markets. One night something got into the henhouse, apparently by breaking the lock, and took 21 chickens. There was no evidence of blood, bones, or feathers that would indicate any struggle. The only evidence left on the premises were some very large footprints in and around the entrance way. It is hard to believe that someone or something could so silently take 21 hens without leaving a trace. One would have initially thought it was a local group of teenagers, but when massive footprints were found, that idea quickly changed.

In the fall of 20**, an apple farmer in Washington State named Zach Bell tells of his Mackintosh orchard being raided overnight on the eve of the harvest. Hired migrant workers went to the fields early one day to pick from the 400-tree farm, only to find that a large number of the trees had been picked bare. These same trees were full of ripe apples the day before. Who or what could take about 200 bushels of apples from trees in a matter of hours during the night -- and without making a sound?

The next night, Mr. Bell went into his orchard with a flashlight to make sure his grounds were secure. It was then that he saw several very large dark shapes moving along the tree line of the orchard. He immediately went back into his house and called the authorities.

Elsewhere in the state of Washington, a husband and wife recently had a very interesting Bigfoot encounter. One autumn night with a bright harvest moon in the sky, the couple heard a disturbance in the back of their farmhouse. The couple had been experiencing these sounds for several days, yet they never saw anything that caused any suspicion or fear. But on this particular night there would be more than just sounds and definitely something to fear. When the husband exited out the back door of the house to investigate why his several hound dogs were barking, he got the shock of his life. A large Bigfoot was standing half in and half out of the shadows beside his garage.

The creature was swaying back and forth and staring directly at the man at a distance of only 50 feet. The man froze; then, trying to stay calm, he slowly began backing up into the house. Once inside he ran for his shotgun and shells. At this time, he heard the dogs crying and a large metallic crashing sound. As he ran outside he saw that the heavy dog kennel was ripped apart. Two dogs were dead, necks snapped, and the other three could be heard yipping and running in the dark back fields. The Bigfoot was nowhere to be seen, but its powerful stench remained. The couple immediately contacted authorities. Official government protocol was followed to the letter. Questions were asked, photographs were taken, statements were signed and property was searched. The authorities at the scene firmly told the couple to remain silent of these matters.

The following stories are a small collection of the most recent experiences that have added to Bigfoot documentation. Each story is unique in its own way, but all are related by verification of witnesses, events being recorded, interaction with government representatives, government manipulation of witnessed events, effort to silence the said event, and lastly, mental and emotional scarring imposed on innocent individuals. The following stories are special, for unlike scores of previous tales that could not be officially legitimatized or validated; these stories are the beginning of a tidal wave of evidence that the government no longer feels capable of containing.

Recent Documented Stories

Documented Evidence # 1235
September 22, 20**, Malheur National Wildlife Refuge, Oregon
Father / Son Camping Trip Encounter

In September 20**, father and son, Dave and Josh Chapman went on a camping trip in the mountains near Malheur National Wildlife Refuge in Oregon. The two had gone to this same camping site for the past three years for their annual father-son weekend that had begun when Josh was six years old. Each year, they took the 2 and a half-hour drive to enjoy a weekend of fishing, swimming, hiking, toasted marshmallows, and, of course a campfire.

Dave drove a large Suburban and had it packed with all the necessities. On the way up the mountain, about 2 miles from their campsite, they passed a ranger's station and a small lake. They arrived at the site and unloaded their gear around 3 o'clock in the afternoon. The Suburban was parked about 50 feet from the tent, just off the dirt road. A trail on the other side of the site was partially overgrown, it forked in two directions: one way leading to the summit of the mountain and the other to the ranger's station.

Part of the weekend ritual for Dave and Josh was going into the woods to collect sticks and logs for a campfire. On this outing, while Josh was picking up sticks and twigs, he found a small tuft of dark brown hair. He showed it to his dad, who thought it was maybe from a coyote or a river fox. After looking at it more closely, Dave thought the hair was a bit too long for those animals, and it also had a somewhat noxious odor to it, not thinking about it anymore, he tossed it away.

After enjoying a swim and some fishing, father and son then settled in for the night. When they woke up in the morning, they found a smattering of debris all over the site. It appeared that they had some visitors in the night, most likely some hungry raccoons. Dave had forgotten to put away all the leftover food and wrappings from what was consumed the night before.

On Saturday they spent a busy day hiking to an area with another small lake, where again they fished and did some swimming. They then went back to the campsite to make dinner. Saturday night was traditional ghost story night, so after a healthy trout and potato dinner, they enjoyed a round of scary stories. Before bed, they made sure all the food and garbage was disposed of, because they did not want a repeat of what happened the night before with their small furry friends.

The tent they were staying in was just the right size for two sleeping bags and a small cooler between them, and it was situated fairly close to the low burning campfire. Around 1 o'clock in the morning, Josh woke up to noises just outside the tent. It was the sound of snapping twigs accompanied by a low deep-sounding groan. Josh shook his father urgently to wake him. They both noticed a pungent smell in the air. Dave immediately thought that the rustling was most likely the raccoons coming around for a second helping of an evening snack. Before going out to scare away the critters, Dave came up with an idea to add a little excitement to their night.

Dave's idea was to splash kerosene onto the fire, light up the area, and then watch the little critters run for their lives. Meanwhile, Josh would record the event on his camcorder. Dave kept a small amount of kerosene in a container just outside the entrance of the tent. He jumped out of the tent, throwing a half gallon of kerosene onto the fire, while Josh turned on his camcorder behind his dad. In a powerful burst, the fire ignited into a mighty flame and engulfed the area in a huge orange glow that lit the campsite for 5-6 seconds.

Shocked, they did not see raccoons, but six large Bigfoot! Two of them were close to the campfire and were driven back by the burst of flame. Another three Bigfoot were peering into the Suburban, and one more was crouching just inside the tree line, observing the scene. The two more startled individuals growled intense groans of fear and at the same time, anger. They had been singed by the leaping flames. Josh, quite shocked at the horrific site, managed to keep the camcorder in motion and recorded the creatures for 6 seconds.

In an act of panic, Dave grabbed his son, with the camcorder, and dashed out of the tent. Unable to go to the Suburban with three Bigfoot blocking the way, the two ran as fast as they could into the woods. Having been fortunate enough to still have a flashlight in his pocket, Dave was able to follow the hiking trail leading to the ranger's station. While running, the two could hear the creatures following behind them, breaking brush, growling loudly, and panting heavily. Bolting through the debris of the thicket, both were scratched and scraped by low prickly vegetation, and they were also forced to slosh through a stream before nearing the ranger's station. Suddenly, both father and son noticed the sounds of pursuit behind them had vanished. With the immediate sense of danger having passed, they rested at the side of the trail with pounding hearts, lungs ready to burst, eyes darting nervously, and ears open for any strange sounds. They rose slowly and moved on, managing to reach the ranger's station without any harm.

Once inside, Dave and Josh notified the park ranger on duty of what they had witnessed. The ranger could see from their physical appearances that they had just been through something traumatic. According to the classified police report, he was quoted as saying, "I could see the fear in their eyes! These two had entered the station breathing heavily, shoes wet and dirty, clothing torn, bodies sweating profusely, and in a heightened nervous state." Dave told the ranger the story in great detail, claiming the most horrific part was to be dragging his son through the wilderness with only a flashlight, all the while hearing the grunting and howling of the creatures that followed closely behind.

The entire time that Dave was explaining what had happened, Josh was sitting still in a chair, not saying a word. His eyes were wide open, staring straight ahead at nothing, and the whole time he held tightly onto his camcorder. At one point in his conversation with the ranger, Dave asked Josh for the camcorder. Josh did not answer, or even look at his father. Dave then gently took the camcorder from Josh's clenched hands. Dave showed the ranger the 6 seconds of film footage, and he was astounded by the incredible images. The ranger called the local police and ambulance services, and within minutes an ambulance came to treat both father and son. At the same time, the local police arrived, accompanied by government officials, who questioned Dave and Josh on their story, and confiscated their camcorder. The two were told firmly not to discuss the event with anyone.

Dave and Josh never again returned to that area of Oregon. Josh has had a series of troubles since that particular night, such as insomnia, refusal to celebrate his birthday in any manner, and also to this day, the smell of kerosene, acts as a trigger to the memories of that terrible night. Actually the smell of any petroleum product will incite panic -- leaded or unleaded.

Documented Evidence # 1767
June 15, 20**, Madras, Washington
6 Women Weekend Encounter

For the past 15 years, six very good friends would get together for a long weekend at a secluded cabin on Lake Billy Chinook near Madras, Washington. These six women would spend their weekend discussing their lives, their families, and their problems over homemade meals and country music. The cabin they stayed in was built on a level lot that overlooked the lake. It was of a smallish square design which was consisting of four rooms, not including a small kitchen and small bathroom. There was a beautiful wrap-around porch with a screen door at the main entrance. Flowering plants and rocking chairs adorned the porch, which made for a homey atmosphere. The place was picturesque and charming, and these surroundings always made for relaxing weekend. All this was about to change.

It was a Saturday evening around dusk, and an early afternoon shower had left a light glaze of moisture on the cabin and surrounding landscape. The sun was just escaping below the horizon, nestled in the mountains that faced southwest. After a nourishing dinner and a few glasses of wine, the women had gathered in the snug living room where they would play a few games of Parcheesi. As was their habit, they had country music playing in the cabin, the volume high enough to be heard, but not loud enough to interfere with the conversation of the six women.

The second game had just started when two of the women suddenly noticed a terrible smell that made them catch their breath. Deloris, one of the more authoritative of the women, thought it was most likely her collie, Sophie. The dog had been outside most of the day, and she had a bad habit of rolling in anything foul smelling that she could locate. She was a very smart dog and would go in and out of the screen door all day by herself. Deloris got up and said "that smell must be Sophie, I'll go put her in the basement," but as she got up she noticed that Sophie had been lying on the floor near her feet the whole time.

Suddenly, the foul odor got worse and the noise of the screen door opening and slamming shut was heard. Sophie began to bark wildly. Then it happened, from around the corner came walking in an eight foot tall Bigfoot. At that moment, the simultaneous screams of six women were heard throughout the valley! The Bigfoot pushed Deloris aside and she was immediately thrown back, hitting an end table with enough force to cause the heavy lamp in its center to topple to the floor.

The creature pushed through the living room. He was an imposing figure; huge, grunting, breathing heavily, exuding a pungent odor, and appearing confused. He started knocking over chairs, lamps and any other items that were at his arm level. The women either scrambled to the windows or crouched down on the floor. They feared for the worst, shaking in their shoes, and crying uncontrollably. The Bigfoot's odor, which smelled of rotting garbage, caused the women to gag, while two of them actually threw up.

Deloris somehow managed to steady herself after being thrown down. She got up, ran to the kitchen, grabbed a large cast iron skillet and went after the Bigfoot, swinging at his head from behind. The blow to the back of its head made a loud thudding sound as the dense metal struck the creature with great force. By the Bigfoot's reaction the impact did not have the effect that Deloris would have wanted. He quickly turned around and with a sweeping motion of his massive arm, clotheslined Deloris and knocked her into a china cabinet full of tea cups. As Deloris hit the cabinet, sounds of breaking china, glass and wood were heard. She crumpled to the floor.

Then, as suddenly as he had appeared, the Bigfoot swiftly turned and headed out the door into the night. The emotionally distraught women called the authorities at once. The paramedics eventually arrived and began to tend to the women. Two of the women were physically injured -- Deloris had a broken clavicle bone from the swing of the beast's powerful arm, and another woman, named Gladys, injured her leg while diving for cover as the creature entered the cabin. The other four women were in shock and mentally shaken.

As the paramedics continued to look after the women, government officials entered the cabin. Rapid-fire questions were barked at all the women, such as, "Was he really that tall? What did he really look like? Are you sure he was covered in hair? How many glasses of wine did you drink tonight?" After the women were debriefed, they were told to not discuss the evening's events with anyone.

The women never communicated with each other again after the incident. Three of the women divorced their spouses the following year, one was admitted to a psychiatric hospital, and two opened up a small family restaurant called "Peggy's

Poultry Pantry," which features an all white meat buffet, every Wednesday night. The following summer, the lake cabin was bulldozed to the ground.

Documented Evidence # 981
March 12, 20**, Redding, CA
Daytime Highway Encounter

It was about 3 o'clock on a bright sunny Wednesday afternoon in Northern California. During a heavy gridlock on Route 5, which runs north to south, suddenly, a Bigfoot appeared out of the thicket and began walking along the freeway. The Bigfoot was an alpha male, over eight feet tall and weighing about 750 pounds. The creature appeared to be trying to get to the other side of the freeway. He seemed confused and a bit agitated as he moved between the slow-moving cars. As he walked, he hit some antennas, bending them, while also bumping into some vehicles. He growled and grunted, as people honked their horns and screamed from their cars, some in fear and some in hope of scaring the creature away. Many cars swerved to avoid the creature and numerous accidents occurred as a result.

While the Bigfoot was causing a commotion on the freeway, three separate people were recording the harrowing events with digital video recorders that they happened to have in their vehicles. Interestingly, the recordings were coming from three entirely different angles, so the video coverage of the creature was excellent. While these people recorded the action, numerous people just stopped theirs cars and jumped out, screaming loudly and running in the opposite direction of the enormous creature. Turmoil and panic erupted on the densely packed freeway, as the sound of people screaming slowly started building.

The creature, at this point startled by the car horns, accident noise, and yelling of people in their vehicles, moved toward the wooded area next to the highway. As he was just beginning to walk back into the tree line, the sound of a gunshot echoed over the turmoil. The shot was not fired by the police, who had not yet arrived at the scene. Rather, a commuter had pulled over in his red pickup truck, aimed his 12 gauge shotgun at the Bigfoot and fired a shot from about 50 feet away. The shot landed directly in the chest of the huge beast! The Bigfoot suddenly paused, disoriented, then dropped to the ground with a strong thud.

The commuter, after shooting the creature, walked slowly toward it with both hands clenched tightly on the gun, keeping it pointed at the downed beast. The shooter's name was Dale Turnplatt, a 6-foot, 250 pound beer-drinking weekend hunter. He slowly bent over the silenced creature and checked to make sure it was dead. The Bigfoot lay deathly still.

People came rushing over to view the creature. Some of them had cameras and they started to take pictures. The expressions on the faces of these witnesses were full of shock and awe. They could not believe the massive specimen that was right before their eyes!

Unbeknownst to the witnesses, Dale, the man who shot the creature, was an extreme pelt collector. Putting down his gun, he pulled out a large, sharp carving blade from inside his boot. He immediately started to carefully skin the creature as if no one was around. The shocked witnesses were silent as he cut straight lines in precise fashion starting below the creature's neck and along its sides. Dale was like a surgeon as he cut in various angles down both legs. He then pulled over and over, and carefully lifted the separated skin from the creature's back and legs. In a matter of only fifteen minutes he had skinned the animals back, legs, and arms. The bedrock was full of blood and tissue from the skinning. Flies started to gather as the dumbfounded onlookers moved in for a closer look.

Four highway patrolmen rushed onto the macabre scene. They quickly gathered up the hunter and the witnesses. The highway area was suddenly awash with patrol cars, paramedic vehicles, and government security personnel. Dale was arrested on the spot for what was deemed cruel and unusual treatment of an animal. When asked why he skinned the animal, he replied that he could sell the pelt for a lot of money, and it would help pay for his mobile home.

Personnel garbed in white protective clean suits, complete with gloves and masks came in with a flat bed truck and carefully packed up the skinned Bigfoot and his bloody pelt. Everything was bagged, labeled and boxed up before it made its way into transport to a highly classified area.

The 86 witnesses in the location of the skinned Bigfoot were shuttled to a secluded area by the government officials. These same officials were combing the area in hopes of shutting off any leakage of information to the outside world. The witnesses were debriefed, per protocol, and told not to discuss the occurrence with anyone. All cameras and video recorders were confiscated.

Dale Turnplatt remains in an undisclosed detainment area, being thoroughly evaluated. Several of the remaining witnesses have experienced a variety of problems such as insomnia, constant nightmares and emotional disorders. Almost everyone present on the highway that day underwent some sort of change in their lives because of the incident.

(Note: Dale Turnplatt, while incarcerated, received an award from the World Wide Hunters Alliance for bagging the first Bigfoot. The award came in the form of a bronze trophy, a bullet key chain, and a life-time subscription to *Carcass Magazine*.)

Documented Evidence # 2653
July 21, 20**, Klamath Forest, Oregon
Lindsey Footage

In July 20**, the young botanist, Lindsey Phillips, was doing research in the Klamath Forest of Central Oregon. She had driven up ten miles of mountain dirt roads in her Jeep Wrangler and had been at a secluded campsite for four days. She was planning on staying for about two weeks, with the hope of documenting local plant life with her digital camera. Although she was having a good time doing research on something she loved, she was battling a bad cold at the time. Other than that, she was your ordinary camper, with a typical tent, a fire every night, a packed surplus of food and drink, an iPod and a digital high definition camcorder.

One morning about two hours after sunrise, Lindsey had just finished picking up the campsite from a small meal she had just made. She was planning on going over some notes she had been taking the day before when she decided she would go down to the lake and take some digital footage of the morning sky. The lake was about 800 yards from her campsite. She walked down and sat on a large rock by the water shooting some scenic views when she heard some sounds coming from her campsite. She thought it might be some wildlife fishing around for something to eat, so she figured she should go back and investigate.

As she approached the site, all looked calm. She neared a large Douglas fir that was about 15 feet from her tent. This enormous tree was about 700 years old, and had a trunk that was about 4 feet in diameter. Just as she passed the fir tree she suddenly noticed a gigantic hairy Bigfoot backing out of her tent! She suddenly gasped for air and backed up quickly behind the huge tree to hide. With great presence of mind she turned on her digital recorder and peered around the tree, pointing the camera toward the creature. To her surprise, the large creature did not appear to notice her, although she thought he did see her when he came out of her tent.

With calm demeanor Lindsey kept the camera steady as she recorded footage of the Bigfoot reaching in and out of her tent, grabbing her knapsack and her sleeping bag, shaking them around, and looking curiously at everything. The creature was enormous in size at over 8 feet tall and weighing over 700 pounds. He had dark brown hair that was tufted in various areas on his body. She was at a distance of about 15-20 feet getting crystal clear footage as the creature meandered around her campsite. While she was filming, the Bigfoot glanced over to Lindsey on numerous occasions, recognizing that she was present, and that she was not an imposing threat. He did not at any time use any type of aggressive behavior towards her.

While rummaging through the site, the Bigfoot found some food in a cooler and started to eat it. Lindsey carefully zoomed in on the animal and recorded his mannerisms as he broke open plastic bags of items and stuffed clumps of food into his huge mouth. Being a woman of science, she carefully panned into his body closely, recording such things as his articulate muscle movement, the encrusted fecal matter on his backside and thigh area, a close up of his feet, the palms of his hands and several close ups of his face. The sound of his breathing had a deep guttural tone, something she had never heard before. In later interviews, Lindsey stated she was extremely nervous but she understood the importance of the footage, and what it meant to the scientific community.

At one point during the recording, Lindsey had a short coughing fit, most likely induced by the creature's incredible stench as by her cold. The Bigfoot seemed to become mildly agitated from the noise and suddenly halted his rummaging through the campsite to peer directly at Lindsey. He then displayed a swaying stance and rumbled with a low growling noise.

Lindsey was keen to the creature's change in behavior so she slowly began to retreat to her Jeep which was parked nearby. She carefully slipped into her vehicle, still allowing her camera to record the Bigfoot. After Lindsey was locked in her vehicle, the male Bigfoot approached and peered inside at her. When it realized that she was secure inside, he very lightly rocked the vehicle. The creature must have understood that Lindsey was not a threat by her submissive behavior. One can only wonder what would have happened if she had honked the horn or made any type of wild gesture, or upset the Bigfoot in any way. Suddenly, the Bigfoot became distracted and quickly turned away when he saw a brightly colored antenna ornament. Then, without warning, almost with a manner of disgust, he walked away into the thicket with Lindsey still in her vehicle panting heavily.

With this encounter and film footage, so much was gained. We can clearly establish the true size and the unprecedented physical breadth of this creature. Critical undeniable evidence was also left behind such as Bigfoot saliva which was found on granola bar wrappers, hair samples from various items in the campsite, and footprint castings which were made from impressions left in the area.

Unlike the previous 1967 16mm footage, which had been questioned and challenged for decades, this amazing footage would take the Bigfoot interest to another level. This footage ran for a full 21 minutes in crystal clear definition, taken from 20 feet away (2-3 feet when Lindsey was inside her jeep). This would even prove to be better than the confiscated footage taken on Route 5 in Northern California during the daytime Bigfoot sighting.

This film would become known as the famous *"Lindsey Footage"* and it would prove to be the most important footage ever shot of Bigfoot's existence. It also single-handedly began the current Bigfoot hysteria.

After Lindsey Phillips recorded "The Event", she immediately sent the footage to several colleagues at her university; and then, sensing the importance of this information to the world, she downloaded the footage onto the Internet. The clip went viral and became an overnight sensation. It was now official that Bigfoot was real and he was a valid entity. He was no longer in the shadows. He was right on your computer monitor, live and in full color. This broke everything wide open! The government could not contain this information or "debrief" the clip's worldwide viewers. In a matter of minutes, Bigfoot perception was changed by the dissemination of the *"Lindsey Footage"*.

This was also a turning point as far as finally having valid, clear, precise visual evidence that showed Bigfoot. This was the evidence that forever changed how the government was to view Bigfoot as well. The video released to the public created such a stir, that the government had to now reevaluate its approach on dealing with the information the public was getting on *Gigantopithecus karakus*.

The actual camcorder that Miss Phillips used to make the historic video just recently went on auction in New York City. The winning bid came from a wealthy and eccentric land developer in Florida, for a price of $217,000.00. This individual, who chose to remain anonymous, has a very diverse collection of oddities from around the world. Part of this collection consists of a piece of a unicorn's horn, nine scales, supposedly from the Loch Ness Monster, and a pair of leprechaun shoes.

(Note: it must be stated that the leprechaun shoes do in fact come with a letter of authenticity)

SECTION 2

Interviews

Dr. Angus Maddox, PhD – *Head of the BF Eco-Habitat and Langley Facilities*

Meadow Greene, DVM – *Co-Founder of the Coalition for the Protection of Bigfoot*

Modern Technology Validating Past Historic Events

It is unorthodox to have interviews in a government manual, but we believe that it would be more personable for the public to read the actual interviews from key people in the Bigfoot edification program.

Interview with Dr. Angus Maddox, PhD

- Head of BF Eco-Habitat and Langley research facilities
- Master's degrees in Mass Communication, Business Admin., and Zoology from the University of Texas
- Doctorate of Paleontology from Yale
- Author of: "Large Mammals of the Dark Continent", and "Fossils from Tomorrow"

Interviewer – Stuart Plainview
Date: 1:13 p.m., November 2, 20**

Plainview

Good afternoon Dr. Maddox, thank you for giving me some of your precious time. In your own words, could you tell me about the two Bigfoot facilities in the Cascade Mountain area of Oregon, and Langley, Virginia?

Maddox

Good afternoon Mr. Plainview, it would be my pleasure to discuss the two research facilities. The one in the Cascade Mountains was the precursor, the first research facility opened exclusively for the containment and study of this creature. This facility is now known as the BF Eco-Habitat. The location was originally going to be a military site, but they lost their funding in 1971 and it was then taken over by a sub-division of the government.

The Langley facility located in Virginia is a highly guarded, highly technical facility. The more specialized equipment is located there. We tend to do more work on the bio-medical end there, and we can do more fine tuning with the equipment that we have available at Langley.

Both facilities were started about seven years ago. This was due to the onset of more video imaging, pictures, encounters, and sightings of Bigfoot. There were a lot of these sightings we could not contain anymore. We needed to obtain a Bigfoot, and we did obtain one, in 20**. He was brought to the Cascade facility and we named him Buster. He was captured as a result of a rock slide in Oregon. We found him unconscious. He was a very large alpha male and was brought to the Cascade facility. So, that's how it all began. We learned a great deal from having Buster in our facility. We also made some mistakes, but it has all been positive. And again, at Langley we are fine tuning our bio-medical work there.

Another aspect of the work we do is related to the capture of Bigfoot in the wild. The detainment of Bigfoot away from its environment is both difficult and treacherous for the creatures. Novice handling can lead to unnecessary negative end results to these creatures. Some methods used to obtain Bigfoot can vary among certain areas of the country, and the safety of our personnel is always our number one priority. Research facilities should make sure that anyone trapping Bigfoot should be properly trained and aware of illegal methods of obtaining a specimen. The practice of killing a mother to acquire an infant is sometimes acceptable. If this does occur, the carcass of the mother can still prove to yield much valuable information.

Question

How many creatures are at each facility?

Maddox

There are thirteen creatures at the BF Eco-Habitat and five at Langley.

Question

Any problems keeping them confined at these facilities? It

seems like there is more space at Langley.

Maddox

Langley is three times the size of the BF Eco-Habitat. Langley is a more medical and technical facility, and the equipment is much more sophisticated. This is also a much more secure site, and as I said, more involved testing and analysis can be done there. At the BF Eco-Habitat, it is more of a natural habitat set-up, and we do a lot of initial studies there, somewhat rudimentary work, but with other bio studies needed, we moved to Langley for more advanced work.

The BF Eco-Habitat is actually a very impressive, spacious, natural, serene setting. We would typically take the newly captured Bigfoot into this site, do initial prep work, light studies and evaluations, and then eventually move the more advanced specimens over to the Langley site for more advanced analysis.

Question

Being at the forefront of this discovery, what has been the biggest hurdle for you, to date?

Maddox

We have not experienced any problems with the study of the creatures, per se, other than a few minor situations with agitated, unruly creatures. Within the first month some technicians did get hurt and actually two technicians were killed. We had some trouble separating some family groups, or pods, as we call them. I remember there was this one particular group that was composed of one large male, two females, and three offspring. The male became extremely violent, and as we tried to confine and sedate him, he lashed out and killed two technicians with the swing of his arms.

We look at this as part of a very big learning curve, as it was very difficult getting the creatures accustomed to their new environment. We lost a few Bigfoot in the beginning, maybe five or so. They did not take well to being in captivity. Some did not eat and some were very, very agitated. So I would say one of the biggest hurdles was that in the very beginning of the learning process, it was difficult for the Bigfoot to adapt and understand what we wanted from them.

But now things are much different. We have gained so much information; we know where we are going, what our plan is, and how we can obtain what we need.

Another item I should mention would pertain to the general public, as they have been somewhat disruptive and putting up a lot of road blocks for us. Animal rights groups like the *"Coalition for the Protection of Bigfoot"* have been getting in the way by picketing our Langley facility, trying to prevent vehicles from entering, putting negative information on the internet, and a host of other things. So I guess I can also say that this has been as much of a hurdle as learning about Bigfoot was for us, initially.

Question

How did you handle these creatures without their massive size causing issues? What means did you use to keep them in line?

Maddox

In the beginning we used heavy clubs and cattle prods. This was the only way to keep them from hurting a lot of the workers; of course there were occasions where we did have people get hurt or killed as I mentioned earlier, but these methods were not very effective. These creatures are about 700 pounds and we really needed a better way to keep them in check.

So we needed to up the ante, and went out and got some of our military people involved from Langley. We developed the BF Crippler; the taser designed for use with Bigfoot. I am sure you are aware of what this is. This taser really solved all our issues with violence in Bigfoot; it took our training to a whole new level, and really helped us to control these creatures.

Question

Could you speak a little more about what exactly the BF Crippler is?

Maddox

It is actually a handheld taser with extreme power. If this were used on a man it would kill him instantly. When used on a Bigfoot, it will stun him very nicely and has proven to be a very effective tool in managing this creature. The initial prototype developed by our military engineers was worked on and tested for months until they came up with a very unique design that is light, easy to use, and is extremely powerful.

Question

How many people are involved in the Bigfoot Edification Process in the gathering of all this information?

Maddox

We have 57 in the BF Eco-Habitat and 112 in the Langley site. These are all full-time government employees, all hard-working people that the government is proud of. They are all highly trained and college educated, holding a wide variety of advanced degrees and special backgrounds.

For example, we have Paleontologists, Anthropologists, Primate Specialists, Mathematicians, Behavioral Scientists, Mass Communications Specialists, Psychologists, Sociologists, and so on. Like I said, we have a wide variety of highly skilled people who help us look from every possible angle at how a Bigfoot is put together and how they function -- physically, mentally, and socially.

Question

I am sure you are aware of the government manual that is being created and that most of this content is being gathered from work done at the Cascade and Langley sites. Could you expand on this?

Maddox

Well, it is a very important document and yes, it needs to be constructed. A great deal of the information for this manual has been gathered through our testing done at the two research facilities. This manual is a very important piece of documentation, and it is being put together based on the public outcry for information regarding Bigfoot. It is something they have demanded, and they are looking for direction and understanding of this creature. By publishing this manual they will be getting the pertinent information we think they will need in order to feel secure.

Question

For these sites, what would you consider to be immediate and future goals?

Maddox

Well, the objective is the same for each site, that being to gather as much insight and information as possible on these creatures. Yet the main goal is to keep the public safe and educate them, and also possibly understand more about ourselves from studying them.

Question

Could you tell me more about the Bigfoot species based on testing and studies done at both facilities?

Maddox

Well, a lot of the information gathered is highly classified, but I can tell you we are dealing with a very strong bipedal omnivore. We have done strength testing on this creature, and every one of these tests has come back with amazing results. A lot of people do not know that the Bigfoot creature can run very fast. We have clocked one Bigfoot at Langley who can run up to 33 mph.

There are a lot of things we cannot get into. We are gathering information every day. The best way for the public to get any declassified information will be from the manual when it is published.

Question

Would you consider keeping Bigfoot confined in captivity a measure of National security? Are we trying to keep these creatures away from the public? My understanding is that the government has these large confinement vehicles that go into areas and take Bigfoot away from public areas when they show up, and then bring them into your secure facility.

Maddox

The containment vehicles are used to go into public areas; they were designed strictly to obtain a Bigfoot, mostly at night. These vehicles are very high tech, highly reinforced, and are used to collect a Bigfoot in the wild or when they become unruly in public areas. These specialized vehicles are called BF Juggernauts.

Question

And in regards to the issue of National security?

Maddox

Well, we are looking at a creature, a relatively unknown

creature until recently, that is extremely large and roaming throughout our mountain ranges. I think the country should be alarmed, and they should get answers. We are talking about a very powerful creature, and they have no public information yet, so the government has to step in and provide this information. We feel that this will offer the security which the public demands.

Question

Do you have any interesting stories that you would like to share, maybe from the early days, while interacting with these creatures?

Maddox

No, there are none that have been declassified beyond what we have discussed.

Question

On a lighter note, is it true that you named the first Bigfoot brought into captivity after your cat?

Maddox

Yes, this is true, my cat is….. well, my cat *was* a calico. His name was Buster and he was actually in my Jeep when I received the call that an unconscious Bigfoot was found in a rockslide. He was there in the beginning years and was with me when we started up the Eco-habitat. Buster had the run of the facility, and everyone knew him, but there was an unfortunate microwave incident, and he is no longer with us. He has since been replaced.

For the purpose of appearing balanced and fair, a second interview from an opposing viewpoint has been included.

Interview with Meadow Greene, DVM

- Co-Founder of the *Coalition for the Protection of Bigfoot*
- Certified Veterinarian
- Animal Rights Activist
- Vegetarian
- Author of: "Aromatherapy and You"

Interviewer – Stuart Plainview
Date: 10:45 a.m., November 14, 20**

Plainview

Can you tell me why your group was formed?

Greene

We are the *Coalition for the Protection of Bigfoot*. The group was formed by my associate David O' Tool and myself back in September 20**. We started looking at all the evidence concerning Bigfoot and talked with many individuals who had experienced encounters. It was at that time that we realized the urgent need to protect these defenseless creatures. Believe me; we are dealing with a very peaceful and very docile creature here, which to our knowledge has never in our history harmed or hurt anyone. We feel that this species does not need to be studied. They do not need to be misrepresented, or put under a magnifying glass and tainted by our government.

We feel this creature should roam free, just like any other natural creature in this country, and I truly believe that this creature is closely related to us humans on the line of life. I believe we are directly related along an evolutionary path, and at some point hundreds of thousands of years ago, human and Bigfoot took different evolutionary roads.

We have heard a lot of stories that have come out of the Cascade facility and Langley that quite frankly indicate heavy abuse towards this species. The authorities at these sites are very quiet and tight-lipped. They will not discuss or divulge specific information about what goes on in these research institutions, and they will not allow us to come in and view these facilities. There are a lot of secretive things being done there, not only during the day, but also at night, and all my organization wants are answers from these officials. We want them to tell us what they are doing and we want to make sure that this creature is not being abused, harmed, or treated negatively in any way.

Question

So you feel the government should be under observation?

Greene

We feel that the government is not following certain guidelines and laws that have been put in place for a new species such as *Gigantopithecus karakus*. Management practices for Bigfoot require specific care and shelter needs that take into account their physical, psychological, social, and behavioral well being. Increased Bigfoot awareness has resulted in the need for guidelines accepted globally for Bigfoot acquirement, care, and experimentation. In this way we can ensure that these creatures are cared for in an appropriate manner when any type of experimentation is performed on them. Due to various differences between countries, guidelines need to be standardized in order to attain acceptability, regardless of these differences.

Consequently it is our aim to provide a stratagem that works to ensure execution of appropriate standards for the care of Bigfoot.

Question

What do you feel is the biggest problem in taking Bigfoot captive?

Greene

The Bigfoot in the wild are under increasing pressure due to the destruction of their habitat and by human encroachment. The government has gone out and captured free living Bigfoot for reasons they justify as scientific, general curiosity, public threat, and other fictitious reasons not mentioned here. These reasons go against animal welfare guidelines set up for the protection of a threatened species. Government officials feel it is within their best interest to capture or confiscate these creatures, they feel it is justified and within scientific reasoning to examine, probe, and evaluate them. Once this is accomplished they will then discard the Bigfoot, like a used car that no longer runs.

Question

Please give me a breakdown of your organization's rules for containing and working with a Bigfoot upon capture.

Greene

We feel that all Bigfoot should be free and that containment facilities and habitat areas should not be in existence. We realize that the government will have its way and all my organization can do at this level is try to report any obvious neglect, abuse, or cruelty. With regard to containment, most newly acquired Bigfoot that are held in the field should be kept in a holding area that promotes calmness and serenity. The compartment size should be of suitable space for the size of the creature, so as not to constrict and eliminate free movement in vertical and horizontal directions. If the compartment is a cage of some sort, this should be elevated off of the ground to allow urine and excrement to exit out freely. For a reduction in Bigfoot trauma, compartments or caged enclosures should be put together for captive family members. The detained Bigfoot should not be put into human dwellings. Exposure to human pathogens could pose serious threat to newly acquired captives.

Also upon capture, Bigfoot should have access to species-appropriate food and water. This should be provided on a continuous basis. The introduction to non-native foods should be avoided, but if this is not an option, then new food introduction should be gradual, and highly monitored.

As I just mentioned, the Bigfoot could be highly susceptible to disease-laden pathogens when captured. This could occur due to stress and possible human exposure. Sickness and death may result due to this exposure. Strict precautions should be taken to avoid endangering the captured creature.

Question

Can you talk about how the Bigfoot should be transported to a facility, and maybe expand on what should be done once they arrive?

Greene

During transport, a Bigfoot's anxiety level will be extremely high and thus, injury could result if precautions are not taken. Acclimation to the vehicle and/or container in which they are transported is important to the well-being of the captured Bigfoot. Minimization of stress is a key factor in getting the creature to its final destination. As a last resort, if a Bigfoot becomes unruly and hostile, a sleeping dart should be used to put the creature to sleep for the trip duration. I know that our government uses a special containment vehicle called the "Juggernaut". This crafty high-end box container is nothing more than a glorified "prison on wheels". I think it should be banned!

Once the Bigfoot arrive at their final destination, they should be supplied a housing facility that will have adequate security built in to protect against any type of vandalism, whether internal or external. There should be adequate secondary enclosures or containment barriers built into the housing area, in the event that a creature does escape. The living area should be large enough for Bigfoot to interact with other captive members, and it should have the feel of a natural landscape.

Human contact should be minimized, more so during the initial introduction. When interaction is needed it should be limited to professionals trained in working with Bigfoot. Medical personnel should be available in case of accident, injury, sickness, or death.

Keeping compatible Bigfoot pairs together is an important part of social structure and that should not be disregarded. There are instances where housing groups together is not possible, so the best alternative is to put compatible pairs together. Single caging should only be considered as a last resort. If there is no other alternative, then it should be short term and under Bigfoot specialist supervision. Human interaction should not be considered an alternative to social needs of the Bigfoot.

Question

Could you elaborate on what a suitable living habitat should be for Bigfoot?

Greene

The environment should encourage a Bigfoot to carry on typical complex daily functions. The living area should provide a sense of security and have adequate stimuli to allow the Bigfoot to exist comfortably and naturally. The physical space that a captive Bigfoot is placed into should have proper lighting and a controlled light/dark cycle that emulates his natural environment. This is very beneficial in creating a positive environment for the creatures.

Another factor to consider for Bigfoot well-being is to keep sudden or unexpected noise to a minimum. The Bigfoot has a very sensitive eardrum which is similar to that of a dog. They can hear high-pitch sounds that a human cannot hear, and they should be kept away from places that could create these types of sounds, such as refineries, chemical plants, manufacturing areas, wind turbines, and evacuation sirens.

The Bigfoot is considered a relatively clean creature based on what data we have from field studies. So when they are brought into captivity, it is essential to provide a sanitary environment for them to live in. This would include any enclosed areas, cages, containment zones, and in both indoor and outdoor facilities. Precautionary care should be used in cleaning these areas which Bigfoot have resided in, as the Bigfoot can be susceptible to reactions with industrial cleaners, detergents, and various disinfectants. This should also be considered when transporting Bigfoot from capture via containment vehicles such as the BF Juggernaut. Bigfoot has been known to "mark" his area by emitting a scent from the Palmbulbus gland located at the base of the spine.

According to studies, this scent is extremely difficult to eradicate from a marked area. In fact the scent should not be totally removed from a cleaned housing area as the Bigfoot has exhibited more behavioral issues when brought back to a totally sanitized area versus a partially cleaned area. As part of keeping the areas cleaned, we must keep in mind pathogen potentials. These need to be kept to a minimum not only for the benefit of Bigfoot, but for facility personnel as well.

Question

Are there any other items that you care to discuss?

Greene

Yes, records and information that is coming from the data gathered on this new documented species need to be maintained and shared with all. Data should be regularly updated, as it is essential for Bigfoot upkeep. Information should be kept on individual creatures such as sex, date of birth, height, weight, temperament, training records, social status in group, and any history that is pertinent to the individual. Also listed should be all medical data, such as injuries, surgeries, vaccinations (if any), breeding habits, partners, offspring, etc. If a Bigfoot is moved from one facility to another, their records should go with them. What I'm talking about is the basic relaying of information that is going to be so vital for the survival of this creature, which brings me onto the topic of breeding.

The only acceptable method for providing a future supply of Bigfoot is through captive breeding. In this way, we guarantee an ample number of species that will be available for medical, experimental, zoological and analysis needs. Propagation in captivity ensures suitable breeding stock, and is more appropriate than going into the wild to obtain more species. Captive breeding should only be done by facilities with proper equipment and trained personnel.

A population control plan should be properly instituted and followed, to ensure the health and the well being of the species population. All breeding programs should be similar to what is occurring in the wild. Common system breeding platforms should follow the quality practice by using the healthiest Bigfoot that are available. These Bigfoot should be selected based on such genetic qualities as health, behavior, temperament, disease status, reproductive performance, and parenting traits.

Question

You have commented on various government shortcomings and of government legalities, but what of your own group? Are you aware that your group is breaking laws while you are organizing protests and interfering with a government research facility? We have heard of altercations at the Langley site and the disruption of government work there. Can you comment?

Greene

Well yes, we are very passionate about what we do. We know there are improper activities going on, and we want answers. Yes we have gone to this facility, and yes we have camped out, and yes we have picketed, and yes we have contacted the media, but you can't make an omelet without cracking some eggs. We need to be here and be disruptive.

This outcry is for the Sasquatch, or Bigfoot, as they cannot speak for themselves. They need a voice, and we are their voice. There are laws on the books that have been put in place to protect all creatures, but we feel that these laws are being overlooked. There are animal rights protection acts in place to do only one thing, protect these creatures!

We feel they are being victimized, so if we are breaking the law, we are looking at the greater good. That being said, it still hurts when we read some of the names that my group is referred to on the internet, such as "Nerds for Bigfoot", "Sasquatch Squatters", and the painful "Stink-bombs".

Question

Could you tell me how you obtain funding for your organization? You are a private group and it appears you have a substantial backing based on the size of some of the protests and organized rallies witnessed.

Greene

No comment! But I will say that we do have some friends such as actors, musicians, celebrities, and others. We have also received influential support from other parties with a lot of money, who have given generously to help our cause.

Question

What type of effect do you see that your group is having as far as pushing for Bigfoot rights?

Greene

What will be interesting is what we will see when the government comes out with their manual. We are somewhat nervous about this manual, and what content will be handed to the public. Will it provide the vision they suggest? What will the immediate effect be? We hope it does wake the public up. We want people to know that these creatures do have rights.

We've heard horrible stories of people collecting Bigfoot hides, skulls, making ashtrays out of Bigfoot feet. We've heard stories from Langley about electric shock being used on these creatures for teaching purposes. That's what they call it -- "teaching." There are stories of starving Bigfoot, separating pods. We've heard horrible stuff, so we want the public to know that these are some of the things that are being done to Bigfoot. This is a docile creature that has roamed this country a lot longer before man ever got here. These creatures probably have more rights to this land than we do!

Question

Why doesn't your group try to work with the government? Have there been any times when you have tried to work together?

Greene

We have tried to work with them on several occasions, and all we've met was a wall. The government does not want to work with us or deal with us. They wish we would close up shop and go away. Now when the government sees us, we just get arrested for a number of false ludicrous violations that they make up on a daily basis. It is ridiculous how they treat us, as we are only fighting for the rights of a defenseless creature.

Question

You seem angry.

Greene

Because a lot of the work we do has been pushed aside and we're not reaching the amount of people we had hoped we would. We have been silenced in the media by the government. We have had information on the internet mysteriously pulled off for no apparent reason, and we have had web sites squashed. We believe this is all being done by the government. Yes this makes us, all of us, very, very angry and bitter! We are trying to do something based out of passion and purpose. We are not doing this thing robotically just for gaining information on these creatures, like dissecting them. We're doing this because we believe there are tragedies happening with some of the studies being done to this creature. Yes there are moments that this group is angry. We try to turn that anger around and turn it into positive energy, its all about protecting these creatures.

Question

One last question… I have met several people in your group besides yourself, and it seems to me that the one common element that connects you people, besides feeling that Bigfoot needs your protection, is your apparent total disregard for personal hygiene and basic grooming. Could you shed some light on this?

Greene

No comment!

Modern Technology Validating Past Historic Events

When using sophisticated modern technology in looking at past Bigfoot information, convincing data has revealed and confirmed that several of these events were indeed real.

Skookum Cast Evidence

Footprint castings have always been an excellent piece of physical evidence for Bigfoot researchers. These castings, which are larger than that of a human being, can show dermal ridges and inclusions. In addition to "normal-sized" Bigfoot prints, there has even been a casting of a crippled Bigfoot print. The most unusual and controversial casting ever generated would be the Skookum Cast, which recently has been one of the more important "castings" of a Bigfoot ever discovered.

In September of 20**, several men with the Bigfoot World Researchers Organization went into the Cascade Mountains in Southern Washington State. The campsite was set up in an area called Skookum Meadows. The purpose of their expedition was to document and detect evidence of Bigfoot. Some of the evidence they had hoped to obtain included any film footage (a fortunate sighting), detailed footprints or tracks, hairs, scat, signs of foraging, and possible vocalization. They had set up some tents on the perimeter of the site which was located near a soft muddy area. They placed some fruit on this muddy area with hopes of enticing a Bigfoot and obtaining detailed footprints. The next morning they went back to this area and noticed a lot of impressions that were definitely not footprints. They felt that they had failed, until one of the men realized that the area looked like a Bigfoot had lain down and reached over for the fruit. It appeared that the Bigfoot had done this with the deliberate intent of not leaving any footprints.

On further examination, another one of the men noticed a very deep semi-circular depression which, at first glance, looked like someone might have pushed a large log into the mud at an angle. The rest of the men gathered around to get a better look and take measurements. The depression, 3 1/2 feet wide by 5 feet long, did indeed seem to be a Bigfoot print, but not the typical flat footprint. The men began to prepare the casting materials. When all was said and done, they had used over two hundred pounds of plaster -- the cast and the information it yielded was intriguing.

What this casting showed was not only the dermal ridges on the sole of the foot, but an impression of the Achilles tendon stretching up from the heel and the actual hair growth pattern of that portion of the lower leg. Due in part to its unique nature, the authenticity of the Skookum Cast has been hotly debated by scientists. There were some rumors that several photographs had been taken of what happened during the night, but everyone in the expedition denied the stories -- until recently.

Only now, many years after the Skookum cast was first made, evaluated and analyzed, do we have solid evidence of its authenticity. A man who will remain anonymous, and is known herein as the "guide," was an expedition worker with the Bigfoot World Researchers Organization. He had taken the men to this location because he knew the area well. His job was to carry equipment cables. He was a sturdy man, well-liked by everyone, and had a great sense of humor. Recently, a government investigation was started by locating and interviewing the people involved with the expedition. Attempts were made to get to the bottom of the rumor surrounding the supposed photographs. Interrogational methods were used when questioning the guide. It was 2:35 on a Wednesday afternoon when this man finally broke down and came clean. What he told us was amazing!

It was a clear, calm night, and there was nice illumination coming from a partial moon. It was about midnight and the guide was in his tent getting ready to call it a night. He heard a rustling sound in the distance, coming from about 60 to 80 yards away. He got out of his tent, not needing a flashlight, but he did grab his digital camera. He moved into the terrain area near the trees and as he got close to the trees where the clearing opened up he saw something amazing and yet terrifying. What he saw was a medium-sized Bigfoot lying on its side reaching over to take and eat the fruit that had been set up in this muddy area by the researchers. The Bigfoot had its back to the guide.

At this point the guide was standing in the tree line about 65 feet away. Remaining completely silent, he focused his camera and took six consecutive photographs. On the third photograph, the Bigfoot reared up slightly, never leaving the ground, and turned to look directly at the trees where the guide was standing. The guide froze in terror. The Bigfoot sat there staring directly at the trees. All of a sudden the Bigfoot lifted its head, smelled the wind, turned back to the trees, and slowly got up, digging its heel deeply into the soil. It walked away to the other tree line and disappeared. As it walked away, the guide lifted his camera and took three more photographs of the creature leaving the premises.

Government officials went to the man's home and persuaded him to give up these photographs. He did not want to show the photographs at the time that he took them, because he was an illegal immigrant. He was fearful that if he brought the photographs forward, there would be an investigation, and his illegal status would be discovered and eventually he and his family would be deported. So he kept the photographs hidden until now and refused to discuss the incident with his wife and family.

When the government discovered what he had in his possession, and then went to his house to collect the photos, the guide made a deal that he would pass them over with the condition that he and his family would not have to leave the country. The government agreed and did get the photos. It should be noted that the quality of the photos was very good, even having been taken at that time of night. They show in full detail and extreme sharpness the Bigfoot lying on its side eating the fruit.

The mystery of the Skookum Cast has been completely solved. The impression was made by a Bigfoot, no question! It should also be noted that the man and his family were returned to their homeland immediately following the receipt of the photos. The event was recorded as solved, closed, and filed by the government.

Ape Canyon Evidence

Another early, more definitive, report of an encounter with an ape-like creature or Bigfoot dates back to 1924. In the Pacific Northwest a group of miners were reportedly attacked by several Bigfoot. This event occurred in an area near Mount St. Helens, Washington.

In July of that year, a group of miners was prospecting in the area. During their days at work the miners had an uneasy feeling, almost like someone was watching them. Later one afternoon, while moving to another mining site, they saw a dark creature peering at them from behind a tree on the edge of a ravine. The men reacted and shot at the beast, causing it to fall over the edge. Later the men searched for the beast and found nothing.

Night was closing in, and the men sought refuge in their cabin, which was located at the base of another ravine. Their horses were tied up and a bonfire burned in front of the cabin. All the men were nervous and they all had their guns loaded that night. The attacks came quickly and with no warning. Huge rocks began showering down on the cabin. Movement in front of the bonfire could be seen through the cracks in the cabin walls. The horses broke free of their ties and ran off. Then the howling and screaming began. The terrified men shook with fear upon hearing the unearthly nightmarish sounds. Shuffling and groaning could be heard outside the cabin walls. The men began shooting through the plank walls out of fear, yet these horrific activities continued throughout the night, and suddenly stopped. As daylight came, the men fled on foot ... for their lives.

As a result of later studies done in and around this area, substantial concrete evidence has been found. Present-day evidence indicates a burial site located near the area where the miners were in 1924. It happened that two hikers found a femur bone that was too large to be of human origin. After the hikers reported the find to local officials, the bone was confiscated and the two men were debriefed.

Upon surveying the area, government inspectors found a cave opening which was closed and protected by a large boulder approximately 200 yards away from the where the miners' cabin had been located. The government brought in heavy-duty equipment and moved the boulder from the opening. The opening led to a natural cave with a long earthen tunnel that went on for about 80 feet before opening up into a cavernous area measuring approximately one acre. Inside this cavern were hundreds and hundreds of Bigfoot skeletal remains. They were neatly stacked and lined up along the cavern walls, which would lead one to believe that Bigfoot intelligence may be of a higher order then we first thought. This appeared to be a burial site, the first discovered and documented Bigfoot burial site. There have been countless sightings of Bigfoot throughout the United States, but never have the remains of a dead specimen been located. Are there other burial areas, or is this a central location for all Bigfoot?

Jacko Evidence

Another story from Bigfoot folklore that has now proved to be very interesting with the application of modern technology is the tale of Jacko, the Minnesota Iceman. This creature, thought to be a young Bigfoot, seemed to have been found by some hunters. It was a male about 4' 7' tall and weighing 127 pounds. It was kept in a railroad car and was fed berries and milk by the hunters who found him. It was handed over to several men who had planned to take him to London for observation and public viewing. Jacko never made it to London. It was believed that the creature died during the passage by sea. Jacko's body ended up back in North America and it was put on display at some state fairs. The attraction caused quite a sensation as it was now entombed in a large cake of ice, then the body suddenly disappeared, but that was not to be the end of this story.

The government became involved and started pursuing the facts. Investigations brought them to Prague. As the layers of the onion were peeled away, one name kept coming up in connection with Jacko. This name was Uri Gravano, a wealthy dentist that lived on the outskirts of Prague. It seems that Gravano had purchased Jacko's body in 1962 from an illegal ivory trader in Africa. How Jacko got to Africa is still a mystery. The body was found in a rundown warehouse in the back of a refrigeration unit, still entombed in the cake of ice that it had been in for many years. The ice had taken on a heavy yellowish appearance and it was deemed from first observation that Jacko was most likely partially-thawed at one time.

The government confiscated Jacko and shipped the creature directly to the facility at Langley. Once there, Jacko was thawed and put through a battery of tests such as carbon dating, bone fragment analysis, DNA-scanning, multileveled X-rays, blood and tissue analysis, anatomy and joint compression, and neuron-extension tests. The DNA-scanning test brought forth some very interesting results.

The data suggests the creature was just a young adolescent at the time of its demise. Bone fragment and tissue analysis both produced basically the same result, that Jacko was nonhuman. There were attempts made to find exactly where this creature was positioned on the tree of life. Structured and multiple level X-rays showed very interesting results in the vertebrae, jaw line, clavicle bone, breastplate, femur, and knee joints.

These observations show distinctive nonhuman traits such as abnormal bone displacement and a wide dense vertebrae column that is much shorter than that of a human of the same size. All evidence at the end of the testing showed that this creature would be considered an uncategorized, undocumented species.

Bluff Creek Film Evidence

Some of the most astounding information comes from the legendary film footage taken by two men in a secluded area in California. These men had a fascination with the concept of a large bipedal creature roaming North America, and one of the men even wrote a book on the subject. They partnered together to try to obtain some concrete evidence of the creature.

They recorded what appeared to be a female Bigfoot crossing a dry riverbed around the Bluff Creek area in California on October 20, 1967. This 16mm film footage has been extremely controversial and the subject of many heated discussions over the years. Scientists from both sides of the Bigfoot fence came out to either defend what was recorded, or to call it the biggest hoax of all time. In fact, the film was so widely known in the public sector that the female creature was actually given a nickname, "Patty" (named after the man who obtained the original footage), and this Bigfoot received as much mystery and fascination as any human celebrity. The footage has clearly been one of the most controversial pieces of Bigfoot evidence to date ... until now.

X-ray Foto-Sensor Imaging

At California Polytechnic Institute in 20**, Dr. Arthur Livingstone, PhD, a pioneer in photo imaging, discovered a startling new method to examine still photos and derive a "heat signature" (HS) from these photos. The process, named X-ray Foto-Sensor Imaging, is a method of sending Nano-Beta X-rays over the surface of a photo and extracting a heat signature based on the time and place the picture was taken. This process was originally designed for the military and was to be used as a means to analyze reconnaissance photographs of "sensitive" areas for heat signatures.

These photos were then reviewed to search for enemy footholds in dense terrain. The process was designed to work with day and nighttime photos. Although it was designed for military use, it has also been used by the civilian population to find lost children in the wilderness. In the past few months, Dr. Livingstone and his team have developed an advanced second generation heat signature analysis system that is now able to pick up different layers of heat such as individual muscles moving, blood flow variation in surface veins, secretions, sweat, and nano-muscular movement.

In Dr. Livingstone's research, he indicates that when a photo is taken and recorded, which could be either a natural still (Polaroid) or a framed type recording, (16mm), each frame gives off a specific heat signature based on electron-neutron re-alignment orientation. This orientation is a result of exposure to a beam of Nano Beta X-rays. Once the photo is exposed to these rays, a signal is emitted. This signal is then uploaded onto a computer and analyzed with software developed by Dr. Livingstone. The result is a heat signature which shows hot and cold areas on the photo.

The technology is so advanced, that it can also pick up heat signatures from objects in the photo as well. For instance, if a woman is photographed in the summer next to a pool, the pool will exhibit a blue scale (low HS), while the woman herself will show a red scale (high HS). Of particular interest is that the technology will show higher HS readings in areas such as the mouth, eyes, armpits, muscles, and even such smaller areas as cuts, bruises, or areas of infection. It should be noted that this technology cannot be used with digital photography.

In late 20** Dr. Livingstone was asked to examine some of the still shots of the famed so-called "Patty" footage. The results were amazing! After running various stills through the process, it became apparent that the heat signatures given off were similar to a photo of a naked man walking down the street. Of particular interest were the muscular areas, buttocks, shoulders, scapula, thighs, back, bottom of feet, palms of hands, mouth, nostrils, eyes, and, also clearly seen, the abscess on the upper right leg!

To prove the worth of the process, Dr. Livingstone needed comparison photos to gauge the validity of his findings. He hired a man to wear a Bigfoot costume and then had pictures taken of him while striding in a way similar to the creature in the film footage. He had this "fake" Bigfoot go through a number of repetitive walks. Countless hours of photos were taken at every possible angle. When a comparison was done, it clearly showed a major difference between what is now considered "real" Bigfoot and a man in a Bigfoot costume. If we were to put the images of the "Patty" material next to the costumed Bigfoot, we would see the following heat signatures:

	Bigfoot Photo	**Costume Photo**
Eyes	Pink / Red	Dark Blue
Mouth	Intense Red	Pale Blue
Nostrils	Intense Red	Pale Blue
Shoulders	Red	Dark Blue
Bottom of Feet	Pink / Red	Dark Blue
Palms of Hands	Pink / Red	Dark Blue
Abscess	Intense Red	N/A
Scapula	Red	Dark Blue

The colors indicated by the results in the table clearly denote that the costumed Bigfoot showed lower heat signatures for most portions photographed, while the "Patty" footage shows high heat signatures with the resulting red hues.

Reinhold Para Scanning

As astonishing as the X-ray Foto-Sensor Imaging method is, what was waiting around the corner was even more astounding -- another new technology called Reinhold Para-Scanning. With this new technology, (named after the man who developed it), scientists and technicians have uncovered the outstanding truth about the Bigfoot footage. This process was developed in North America with government funding, although under a fictitious name. There are currently two sites that are noted for Para- Scanning, one in Utah and the other in northern Russia. Interestingly, after running these facilities for the past five years, it was found that consolidating all Para Scanning into one offshore site was the most logical and cost effective choice. Para Scanning was originally designed for the military.

The twenty-eight feet of Bigfoot film footage examined and tested was a first-generation copy, which was semi-legally obtained from a private source and sent to the facility in northern Russia.

The original film stock used to shoot the footage is considered archaic by today's scientific standards. The photographer's camera was modern for the time (1967) he recorded the footage, and the film stock provided the needed material. The perfect image was there, it just needed to be fully revealed.

The method of Para-Scanning is both a lengthy and a costly process. It is multi- step and can involve up to forty people in order to complete. Initially, it can take up to two months to develop a fully usable product. The complexity is overwhelming.

At the start of the process, the film is heavily saturated in a chemical bath for three weeks. The formula is considered classified and its actual make-up is only known by twelve government technicians. In the second step the film is moved into a pacification unit and gently inundated with ultrasonic waves for a period of two days. This process slowly pulls away at layers of obscuring film emulsion. In the third stage the film is then moved into a mild alcohol buffing fluid. During the fourth stage the film stock is moved into a clear oil-like substance which is again another highly classified formulation. Finally the film is dipped into an alkaline chemical rinse tank. The film is then put through a special digital analysis process and transported to a time sensitive recordable disc. The information obtained from this procedure is nothing short of mind boggling.

After undergoing Para-Scanning, the Bigfoot footage is now not only sharp, but razor-sharp, not only clear, but crystal clear. The creature's face can now be seen in outstanding clarity and with perfect resolution. The heavy brow, bottom jaw, disturbingly deep-set eyes, and conical head are all now perfectly visible. The scanned footage reveals individual muscles moving, as opposed to the unscanned footage, which only hinted at this. A dorsal stripe can now be seen more clearly on the creature. Oil glands can now be observed at the base of the spine. Movement of the trunk, breasts, buttocks, and shoulders now show a much more articulated motion and appear to clearly be nonhuman. The bottoms of the feet are now a mirror image of the plaster castings taken from the area on that day the film was shot. An inflamed abscess can be seen on the creature's upper thigh. Hair growth patterns can be observed more clearly.

Upon viewing this film, one realizes without question that this is not a human in a monkey suit. The enhanced film cannot be seen by the public at this time, as the government has put a highly classified label on its viewing.

(Note: It seems a copy of the modified film was leaked from the Russian facility and found its way to the elite underground. It has been viewed at several secretive locations in eastern Russia. The cost per person for a single viewing has been reported at $12,000 U.S. dollars.)

Russian Containment

Throughout the world, stories of Bigfoot have ranged from simple sightings to events that could never be imagined. Once the government obtained its first historic specimens, it established a Bigfoot research facility in Russia, with the idea of keeping some research on the species out of North America. A secure location has been set up in order to control the dissemination of information to American civilians. To the natives of this town in Russia, the facility is known as the

Moscov Food Processing Plant. With this façade in place, research and study of the creatures has been invisible to the public, including even the transport of specimens in and out of the facility by large containment trucks. These military-owned vehicles appearing with the Food Processing Plant logo, were actually the prototypes for a new line of BF Juggernaut vehicles.

Reports of experiments being performed on the Bigfoot pertaining to aggressive behavior surfaced, creating a negative attitude toward the facility. Eyewitnesses, mainly night janitors, claimed to have observed night technicians putting two aggressive Bigfoot into a large caged area and using stun guns to aggravate the Bigfoot into fighting one another. (Note: these specially designed stun-guns were prototypes for the new BF Crippler). Initially, the technicians thought it would be exciting to watch large creatures battle, but soon, this grew into a version of Bigfoot cockfighting. Seasoned gamblers throughout Europe began visiting the facility on special designated nights to bet heavily, under a cover of secrecy.

This is one reason for a government-backed manual. Man cannot be left to his own judgment or accountability in regards to this creature. What has happened in this small town in Russia could also happen in the heartland of our own country, and provide clear evidence to justify this document. In the past, the government has turned a blind eye to the potential phenomenon of Bigfoot.

Not being at the foreground of the gathering of this information, and in light of the most recent discoveries, hopefully this document will serve to rectify any government misjudgments.

SECTION 3

BF Eco-Habitat

Interview

Dr. Chandler F. Sloan, PhD – *Behavioral Management Supervisor of the BF Eco-Habitat*

Dealing with Bigfoot on a Practical Level
Checklists
Conclusion
Civilian Edification Form

The BF Eco-Habitat, mentioned in the interview previous with Dr. Maddox, is located in the Cascade Mountains in Oregon. What follows is an overview of information that has been ascertained from research, developed and carried out in this facility. The government has chosen to declassify this information in order for the public to be educated in the ways of the Bigfoot. Also included are briefings on new legislation, requirements, and regulations that have been put in place in order to ensure the safety of citizens and their families. Great care and caution has been taken to scrutinize every detail of the behavior and characteristics that have been observed in order to provide the most up-to-date data.

BF Eco-Habitat

The observation/containment facility that has been constructed in the Cascade mountain range is called the BF Eco-Habitat facility. Two Bigfoot family units have the run of this facility, which encompasses an area that is slightly over 3/4 mile long. It is a large climate-controlled dwelling nicknamed "The Bluff" (named after Bluff Creek, location of the famous 1967 film footage), complete with rocks, grass, berry bushes, and even a man-made stream. The complex is kept at a constant 62° temperature with a low humidity level during the day, and 43° temperature at night.

At the research facility there are thirteen creatures (five males, five females, three offspring) that have been studied over 6 ½ years. They have produced some very interesting information. The size and proportions of the individual creatures in captivity are quite varied. The two biggest males are approximately 8 feet tall and 700 pounds, while the two biggest females are approximately 7 feet tall and 550 pounds. The males have a wide chest band, very dense trapezoid muscles, powerful thighs, and sturdy back. The females all have large pendulous breasts, thick torsos and buttock area, and dense shoulders.

The basic social structure of a Bigfoot grouping is called a pod. These pods are a family unit, such as mother, father and offspring or a gathering of several "families" of Bigfoot. These units have been put through many tests and observations in order to better understand who they are and how they live together. Aspects of this published government manual have been based upon studies done on this grouping. Proper techniques and procedures were developed for the manual from these studies.

BF Eco-Habitat Facility Features
(Exact location is highly classified)

o   Completely enclosed habitat – 3/4 mile long by 1/2 mile wide and 92 feet high

o   Special cover material is comprised of a poly-epoxy resin which is air tight, reinforced, and painted with a muted camouflaged pattern

o   Climate, humidity, temperature, and air pressure controlled

o   High tech concealed blowers provide natural air flow patterns throughout the habitat

o   A river flows through the entire site which is filtered and purified daily

o   Natural lighting system is similar to sun's rays, UV / color spectrum

o   8 observation areas

o   Mating cave with pheromone spraying capabilities

o   Unique landscape provides continuous visual interest and stimulation

o   Food items such as fruit, salmon, mice and dandelion greens are supplemented daily

o   Fir trees and edible berry producing bushes populate the habitat

o   Multiple hidden cameras can monitor and record at any time with no blind spots

o   Located just outside the habitat is a separate training facility, discussion rooms, security office and a basic medical center

o   State-of-the-art security system includes retinal scans, voice recognition, and dermal DNA coding

o   Facility garage can hold up to 15 BF Juggernauts

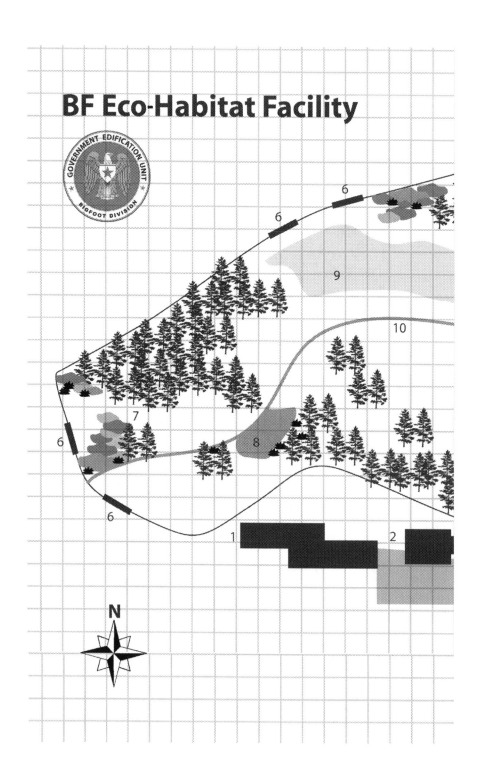

BF Eco-Habitat Facility

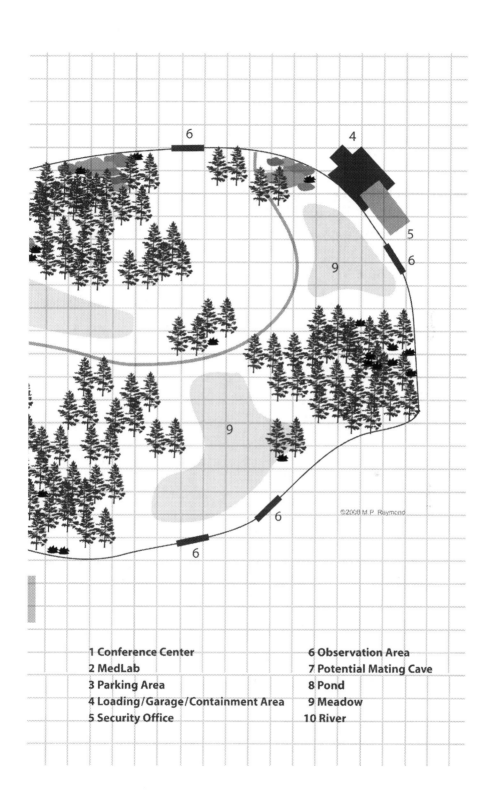

6

4

5

6

9

9

6

6

©2008 M. P. Raymond

1 Conference Center
2 MedLab
3 Parking Area
4 Loading/Garage/Containment Area
5 Security Office

6 Observation Area
7 Potential Mating Cave
8 Pond
9 Meadow
10 River

Natural Habitat

The natural habitat requirements for the Bigfoot species are proving to be very interesting. In the wild they choose to live in tent-like wooded areas, underground or in cave-like dwellings. Several Bigfoot beds have been observed in the wild and they usually consist of fir tree branches laid down on the edge of a clearing. There is also indication that sweet grass or bundled hay placed on small sized rocks has been used. It has been determined that the Bigfoot will nest near streams or other water lined areas about 80% of the time. It can also be noted that on several occasions the Bigfoot has been observed defecating into moving water. We are not sure if this is to hide their evidence of themselves, or if this is to rid waste from their living area. This may be one of the reasons why over the years there has never been concrete recorded evidence of Bigfoot "droppings".

Climate and man-made conditions have dramatically altered Bigfoot habitats. The changing landscape, mainly due to heavy construction and logging in the upper mountainous areas of Washington State and California, has altered drainage patterns which in turn have affected the ground water quality. Global warming has altered Bigfoot migration patterns forcing them to move at times of the year when they normally would not. This has resulted in forcing them to store more food for winter. The human encroachment factor has created a major threat to their survival, which has pushed them into areas that they would once never consider........man's back yards!

Bigfoot Family Structure

The Bigfoot family pod typically includes one family leader, usually an alpha male. Even though the male seems to be the leader of the pod, the female is always directly beside him, and she does not take on a submissive role. She tends to be very protective towards her offspring and is constantly foraging for food and grooming her young. They seem to be constantly fighting for mother's attention; when in the presence of the father they seem to behave in a more humble, respectful manner.

While the female forages for food, the male will watch over the young. It has been observed on many occasions that the male is quite attentive to the offspring's needs and actually plays with them, rolling with them on the ground or carrying them on his shoulders. The Bigfoot offspring behave like typical primate offspring and even resemble human children interacting. They play, tease, and torment their siblings as well as their parents constantly. The male sometimes seems to be aloof and wanders about, usually coming back to the pod with berries, apples, or rodents. All these behaviors have been viewed and secretly studied closely with a wild Bigfoot pod in the Cascade Mountains over a period of four months.

Other observations in the wild show the male has been seen at night to be extremely active and can roam sometimes up to 20 miles. He usually moves along the outskirts of their designated territory and sometimes will interact with other Bigfoot. At this time the complete reasons why only the male becomes active during nightfall and details to any possible migration patterns are unknown, as more research is being done in this area.

Once this pod was obtained and brought to the Eco-Habitat facility, the family dynamic shifted and they became more fragmented and dysfunctional. The stresses of the relocation we feel are the reason behind the change in behaviors. Within this group the male leader of the pod became more aggressive to his handlers as time went on, while the female became more and more submissive. She isolated herself from the male and her offspring. Within three and a half months the female and one of the offspring died.

Bigfoot Height / Weight

We can only comment on the height and weight of the Bigfoot creature by what we have encountered so far. The biggest creature we have documented is 8'6" in height, with a weight of 751 pounds. The smallest creature we have encountered up to this point has been 6'3" and weighing only 364 pounds. One can only imagine what the maximum of height and weight are in the wild.

Bigfoot Strength

Strength tests of Buster, the largest Bigfoot at the habitat facility, proved that he was able to lift 885 pounds, and has been seen throwing a 300-pound boulder over 50 feet on several occasions. When we first acquired Buster from the wild, he was put into a temporary holding facility. He began pounding on the 2 inch thick metal door and if it weren't for the BF Crippler, he would have busted through.

Bigfoot Speed

Bigfoot has been clocked at speeds of 33mph. An interesting fact is that females are actually faster than males.

Bigfoot Smell

The smell of a Bigfoot is extremely powerful, produced by glands at the small of the back that run up the spine. The oil secreted from these glands moves throughout the coat of the Bigfoot, distinguishing one Bigfoot from another and helping to wick water off the creatures hair. We also believe the Bigfoot scent to have a very important role in the mating procedure. At times in the wild Bigfoot can be seen rubbing his lower back along trees and also urinating in the area thus marking his territory.

Attempts have been made to remove these offensive oil glands to make working with the creature a little less difficult for the technicians. The removal of the oil glands proved to be disastrous. When removed from a male, he was observed being excluded from the pod and treated as an outcast. At that point the Bigfoot refused to eat and force-feeding was administered. In two months that particular Bigfoot died. We have stopped research in this direction. A powerful neutralizing spray is now in the development stages.

Bigfoot Mating

The observation of the Bigfoot mating procedures has been quite fascinating. The male Bigfoot will occasionally posture for the female and show his dominant position over her. The female usually submits but there have been times where the opposite happens. Interestingly enough, they seem to always reach a balance or agreement and a certain level of harmony results. The mating procedures begin with a series of multi-pitched cooing sounds. The male will then walk in large circles around the female, these circles get smaller and smaller as he approaches her, and this will go on for hours.

Then when the male does reach the female there is gentle physical contact around the neck and shoulders in the form of rubbing in an almost massaging like manner. At this time it must be noted that the female emits and even more pungent odor than normal. Copulation will happen three to six times in a 24-hour period. When the actual mating is completed the male is documented as almost always falling asleep.

None of the observed mating has yet to produce a pregnancy. No Bigfoot has ever produced an offspring in captivity so there are still many questions that need to be answered about the birthing process. Much has been done in an attempt to produce a pregnancy. We have tried fertility drugs on the female, trying to promote ovulation. Various pheromones have been introduced into the central air system. We have also separated the male and female for two months in order to create a longing for each other. Shellfish have been introduced into the male's diet. We have gone so far as pumping Barry White music through the habitat's sound system in order to create a mating mood. From initial observations, it appears that a Bigfoot male and female mate for life.

Resistance to Communicable Diseases

Intensive tissue studies have shown that Bigfoot's blood has some very interesting properties. DNA testing has also been done at the very beginning of our research which started six years ago, and this has shown Bigfoot to fall somewhere between the mountain gorilla and modern man. The Bigfoot creature seems to be a very strong organism that is almost bulletproof when it comes to disease and cellular breakdown. Now, much work is being done to isolate their organic enzymes and nucleotides in analysis, and is also being looked at in advanced studies with humans.

In our Langley facility we have introduced chicken pox, polio, AIDS, meningitis, and a barrage of other diseases to Bigfoot blood, always with the same results. The blood has remained disease-free. This area of research is getting the most intensive amount of study done and all findings will be released to the public when studies are secure and have been proven over time. One of the many facts still eluding scientists pertains to disease-resistance. Given this condition, how is it that so many Bigfoot have died in captivity? Is it stress, water quality changes, groundwater, air pollution, food substances, changing landscape, or just interacting with man so closely? The government realizes that we still have a lot to learn.

Bigfoot Manure

This particular topic proved to be quite fascinating. One of our security guards at the BF Eco-Habitat enjoyed gardening as a hobby. One evening when he was doing his rounds outside the facility, he happened to be over by the leach field where most of the Bigfoot waste goes underground. He noticed at this point that the vegetation here seemed to be extremely abundant. He asked one of the technicians if he could take home a small sample of Bigfoot fecal matter to try mixing it with soil as he was curious to see how it would work as a fertilizer. The technician felt there would be no harm in doing this and he gave him a sample. The results were amazing.

The security guard planted several vegetable plants in his small greenhouse that weekend. Astonishingly, within three days the plants will already beginning to grow and within two weeks producing vegetables. These vegetables were all incredible in size and quality. Tomatoes were the size of cantaloupes, watermelons the size of garbage cans and so on. All of the information about the potential of Bigfoot fecal matter being used as a fertilizer was kept very quiet by the security guard and the habitat officials were not told of his discovery. The security guard coined the name "Big Stuff" for the fertilizer and began mixing formula for his friends. At this point one of the habitat technicians caught wind of what he'd been doing and the guard was quickly fired.

After this discovery, samples were analyzed at Langley and testing has shown the fecal matter contains large amounts of nitrogen, potassium, and phosphorus. An interesting fact is that this potent fertilizer has more chemical content per pound than your standard industrial fertilizer. New studies indicate that the compound has a built-in release factor that prevents the chemical content from being dissolved too quickly, so you can never use too much. It is a naturally balanced slow-release ultra high-end fertilizer. The fertilizer mixture is actually now in development to be mass-produced for commercial use.

As a result of further research involved with the "Big Stuff" growth compounds, development has come up with a new line of enhanced vegetable products. These products include the "Giganto Tomato", the now popular "Sas-Squash", and a vegetable based white pasta used to make "Yeti-Spaghetti".

Micro-Chip

In the microchipping procedure, a Bigfoot is implanted with a microchip between the shoulder blades. It is then entered into the government data base with a BF MC Series identification number that is specific to that Bigfoot.

With the microchip tracking of a large male in the wild, some information was gathered on the migration of the species. It has been discovered that *Gigantopithecus karakus* is a roaming and migrating creature. Our specimen has migrated up to 300 miles from upstate California to Washington State. It appears that the migration pattern is connected with the changing seasons. In the month of July he was located in Washington State, and then in the month of October he was found to have moved south into northern California. Documented movement has indicated a pattern of moving more frequently at night. It also seems that our specimen Bigfoot and the species in general are very active just before dawn. We are still at this time collecting information on the concept that the migration pattern might be different with an actual pod family unit versus a solitary or rogue individual.

When our microchipped specimen was finally retrieved via tranquilization, several minor wounds in the form of scratches, gouges, and a distinctive limp were observed. We feel this indicates that our specimen may have moved into an area that was already claimed by another Bigfoot, and that perhaps a territorial skirmish possibly resulted. This is conjecture at this point, but we feel it is a possibility.

Vocalization / Communication

Vocalization studies have been observed and recorded in the family pod since the moment of capture. The communication of thoughts, fears, and anxieties can be observed easily. The vocalization consists of clicking and howling, and includes a yipping sound that can hit an extremely high decibel level when the creature is agitated.

One large male in the Langley facility had such a terrifying scream that some of the technicians actually asked to be relocated to another facility in another field of research. Attempts at teaching basic sign language have proven to be somewhat successful. Three of the study creatures can now ask for certain food, water, and have the ability to communicate displeasure or frustration. More research needs to be done in this area.

Storing of Food / Underground Cave

While observing pods in the Cascade Mountain range some other fascinating facts came up about these creatures. They actually store food for the winter months while some pods have been observed to actually migrate to southern areas until winter is over.

Researchers decided to observe one particular pod that chose not to migrate. They lived in a rock shelter, which was observed closely. After the pod moved on, a full analysis of the shelter was taken.

The rock shelter had a series of large grass nests placed toward the back of the shelter. The pungent odor of the creatures was still heavily evident even after the Bigfoot had vacated the area. The workers found stored food supplies such as wild mushrooms, acorns, and wild onions, which were packed tightly against the rock walls. And upon further examination of the dwelling, small animal bones were found. At the time of discovery six years ago, the thought was entertained that they may not be strictly herbivores, but possibly omnivores.

Interview

Interview with Dr. Chandler F. Sloan, PhD

- Behavioral Management Supervisor of the BF Eco-Habitat
- Master's degrees in Behavioral Science and Anthropology from the University of California
- Doctorate of Animal Psychology from Harvard
- Author of: "Primate Now" and "The Mountain Gorilla Index"
- Certified Veterinarian

Interviewer – Stuart Plainview
Date: 4:40 p.m., November 21, 20**

The best way to get the information that is pertinent to the public is to go right to the source for this information, and we believe Dr. Sloan is this person. I was informed just last week that Dr. Sloan would be granting me an interview for the sole purpose and intent of providing undisputed updated information for this manual.

The facility I was brought to is located in an undisclosed location at the base of the Cascade Mountains.

Plainview

Good morning Dr. Sloan, and thank you for giving us the time in your busy schedule for this interview.

Sloan

You're more than welcome.

Question

Please, if you don't mind, tell us a little bit about yourself and the BF Eco-Habitat here.

Sloan

Certainly, I obtained my PhD in Animal Psychology, and prior to that I earned my two Master's degrees, one in Behavioral Science, and one in Anthropology.

As far as information regarding the Eco-Habitat, there is much to discuss. I will try to keep my answers on the subject of scientific information in layman's terms, in order to keep it easy for your readers.

The actual structure of the foundation was erected in the early 1970's. This was originally designed and used as a military base of sorts, but due to limited funding it was closed and the facility was left vacant until eight years ago. At that point in time the government decided that due to increasing sightings of Bigfoot, and some work that was being done at some smaller secluded sites, that a new larger facility was needed. Dr. Maddox was appointed the director of this facility. He was in charge of the massive renovation program to turn the military base into a fully functional, security enhanced, ultra study laboratory, strictly for the purpose of Bigfoot analysis and experimentation.

The habitat itself is approximately 3/4 mile long and a 1/2 mile wide. This is a completely enclosed habitat that is climate controlled to 62° F during the day, and adjusted to about 43° F at night, while humidity levels are constantly maintained. One of the clever features added to this site is a randomized air current system that simulates wind currents. The facility structure has been constructed with a new high tech composite resin that has been impregnated into the concrete matrix. The walls are approximately 2 feet thick and the actual height of the walls is 42 feet. At the very center of the habitat the covering height is about 92 feet high. Inside the Bigfoot habitat there is a flowing stream that is man-made and it runs the entire length of the habitat.

We have found out from observation that the Bigfoot species prefers to defecate in moving water. The stream, as provided, appears to be an excellent natural waste disposal system for the habitat. On the upside, found out in later studies, the Bigfoot fecal deposits are actually beneficial. It appears that the organic compounds contained within their fecal matter have the natural ability to initiate amazing growth results in plants and vegetables.

The habitat has been fitted with a natural lighting system that simulates sunshine and provides for a great source of vitamin D, which is needed by the Bigfoot. Also contained are real rocks and cave dwellings, a natural ledge outcrop, and hundreds of Douglas fir trees that are indigenous to Southern Oregon.

We have even populated the habitat with natural animals such as many varieties of mice, squirrels, and even bird species from the area. A quick note: we found out that Bigfoot loves eating field and deer mice.

Also installed are eight observation areas behind simulated native grass that hides a shatterproof glass wall; each wall being 25 feet wide by 9 feet high. We have also installed the capability to film digitally almost anywhere in the facility. Hidden cameras at various locations in the trees have been placed throughout the habitat. We even have a specially designed mating area for Bigfoot, and we are hopeful that this will one day produce results. This particular area is sprayed with pheromones daily with hopes that it will help to induce a pregnancy.

A concise itemization of our discoveries and observations of the Bigfoot species will be put together into a checklist that will be included in the manual. This I hope will be of help to your readers. In time, by sorting through this information and material using a simpler format, people will better understand the Bigfoot for what it is.

Question

Can you tell us something about the individual Bigfoot that you have here?

Sloan

I would be glad to! We have five males here. Buster was the first to come here and he is our biggest male at 8' 2" and 711 pounds. The second is Tob, and he is 7' 8" and 662 pounds, he was part of a family pod and was the only one to survive the relocation. The third is Skeeter who is 7' 6 ½" and 626 pounds. He is quite a tough one to handle. He is quick to anger and seems to hold a grudge. He has been the most difficult to get through to but we have hopes for him. There are also Nip Nip and Breaker, and you can probably imagine how they got their names. Then of course we have the females Anka, Flux, Sote, Birdy, and Sinmon, and three young Bigfoot, Payee, Kimmel, and Cuda.

They all have unique personalities, are very individualized, and to this day extremely intimidating, the most intimidating being Buster and Tob. In thinking of the Bigfoot stories of the past, one can imagine people seeing these creatures by campfire, or crossing the road, or moving through a field. Most of these images would probably be very nightmarish. There are times that I will see Buster or Tob moving through the habitat in the dark, and the hair on the back of my neck will stand up on end. To this day, I have the same reaction, and I see them every day. It is amazing that even though I work with them constantly, they still can generate the same response in me.

On an interesting side note, the upper officials told us not to give the creatures human names when we started introducing them into the habitat.

Question

Are you working with any other countries in sharing any of

your Bigfoot information?

Sloan

Not at this time… though Russia is extremely interested in our research. We did have a staff technician try to steal confidential papers. It was later discovered that he was a mole and he was trying to steal confidential papers to sell to another country. He has been prosecuted to the fullest extent of the law.

Question

What is your view on the licenses being issued that would allow the public to own a Bigfoot?

Sloan

I feel this is a mistake on several levels. I've talked to upper officials regarding this matter, and it seems to have been ignored. Personally it is a real pressure point for me, but since the powers that be have deemed it appropriate, so be it.

Question

What is going on with the actual training of the Bigfoot?

Sloan

That began very slowly. When the creatures were brought here directly from the wild they were unmanageable, but slowly they began to adapt to their new surroundings and became more workable. Dr. Maddox had someone else involved in a supervisory position at the time and they were using a lot of negative reinforcement in their training and some of it very extreme. We had many meetings on this and these discussions often turned into very heated deliberations, with differing views from all sides.

At one point two Bigfoot died because of this approach in training. The realization finally hit the upper officials that a softer approach would be more effective, although to this day Dr. Maddox disagrees. I am now in charge of the complete facility here and we have been yielding more positive results and moving forward very quickly.

As far as the actual training goes only three of my technicians and myself are physically allowed in the habitat while the Bigfoot are roaming. We do have an enclosed area where we can keep them contained while we clean the facility, but as far as actually working directly with them, only four people are properly trained and allowed to do that.

Question

Was there a break-in at this facility?

Sloan

Yes there was. Someone on the inside knew our security system and was here when we were using negative reinforcement on the creatures. We have laser scan ID cards, retinal scans, and even voice-recognition but they still managed to break in, subdue three guards and then steal the three Bigfoot we had at the time.

We believe they were part of a group that has been actively monitoring our facility, writing negative journals about us, and smearing our research in the mass media. It is believed these creatures were released back into the wild. It was at this point that we introduced the microchip between the back shoulder blades or scapula area of our Bigfoot. It is now a law that any Bigfoot that comes into captivity must be fitted with a microchip.

Question

What is your goal at this facility?

Sloan

We want to truly understand these animals. They were once creatures of legend and myth but now they are in people's backyard. It is important that we gather as much data as we can on their behaviors, such as their temperament, physiology, etc., because I believe that with this information public fear of the Bigfoot will be alleviated.

Question

Do you use BF Cripplers here in your training?

Sloan

Yes, we have BF Cripplers here, but not for training purposes. They are strictly for security reasons.

Question

It's interesting to note and observe the sudden influx of Bigfoot in the country. What is your view on this?

Sloan

Well, I believe there are a lot of reasons for this -- deforestation, air quality, global warming, food source depletion, and human encroachment -- all of these elements and not one by itself.

At this point in the interview Dr. Sloan takes me from our conference room to one of the actual observation stations at the habitat. I get to see first hand this amazing environmental facility. I am completely impressed, it looks like a huge curtain has suddenly been pulled aside and there right in front of my eyes is a little piece of the Pacific Northwest. Trees blow in the wind, birds fly, water moves through the stream, I can even smell the Douglas fir trees. Unfortunately, though, I see no Bigfoot.

Dr. Sloan and I move back to a conference room followed by a technician. Dr. Sloan communicates something to the technician and then we sit down.

Question

I must say the habitat is outstanding. How long was the construction on this site?

Sloan

Construction began almost eight years ago when Dr. Maddox first obtained the foundational section of the building. We realized that we had enough power for our needs, and the construction began within that year. Of course Bigfoot sightings have always occurred, but six years ago was when the influx of sightings began, and the informational sweep began moving through our media. Dr. Maddox and the government in their vision created this training/understanding facility and more importantly, the habitat.

On a side note, I have just been informed that the government has approved and secured property/funding to build five more BF Eco-Habitat facilities. These will be in various locations around the country. Construction should begin in about six months.

At this point in the interview Dr. Sloan is alerted by a beeper in his pocket. He excuses himself, gets up and opens the conference room door. Dr. Sloan has a brief discussion with someone out of view. All of a sudden, I can smell an extremely fowl odor coming from the outside hallway. Dr. Sloan then comes back into the room followed by a technician with a Bigfoot on a chain leash. My heart begins to rise, and panic begins to set in. Dr. Sloan assures me that this Bigfoot is one of the gentler ones and has been slightly sedated. His name is Cuda and he is one of the younger Bigfoot. The Bigfoot stands slowly swaying back and forth looking around the room. I can't take my eyes off this creature. I have never been this close to a Bigfoot. The smell is overwhelming, my anxiety level is sky rocketing and I am having trouble breathing.

Question

Excuse me Dr. Sloan, but I really think you should have warned me that you would be bringing a Bigfoot into the interview. Don't you think that this breaches protocol?

Sloan

(Smiling) Sometimes Mr. Plainview, a head-on approach, is the most effective. Don't worry.... you're quite safe. Say hello to Cuda, *Gigantopithecus karakus* ... one of our adolescents here.

Question

The smell is horrible. How do you and your people deal with this?

Sloan

The smell you refer to comes from a series of glands that is unique to Bigfoot. Interestingly, the odor doesn't bother me as much as it used to. I believe I've been desensitized.

The Bigfoot stops swaying and starts looking directly at me, increasing my uneasiness. Deep set small black eyes, heavy brow, conical head, almost no visible neck, long powerful-looking arms, exceedingly wide shoulders and chest, body completely covered in deep brown, almost black hair. It looks about 6'4" and about 350 pounds. It feels as though the temperature dropped when it entered the room and time was now standing still. I find I can't look for more than a couple of seconds at its face without wanting to leave the room. Suddenly the Bigfoot leans on the table, tilts its head, makes a strange grunting sound and stomps its foot repeatedly. Dr. Sloan whispers something to the technician, who tugs the chain. The technician exits the room with the Bigfoot and closes the door.

Question

What just happened, Dr. Sloan?

Sloan

It seems Cuda felt you were challenging him. I have to apologize; I didn't think he would see you that way. We needed to have Cuda leave the room immediately. It is interesting to note that in the wild, Cuda would have just left the area if you suddenly met. But here in this confined space you became a threat and he was challenged. Modify the environment and you modify the behavior.

This is why it is so important to also study these creatures in the wild, like we did in the beginning seven years ago. We had a pod under observation for four months and fascinating information was gathered. When we acquired several Bigfoot for this facility, I noticed a gradual change in temperament and behavior.

I nod in approval at Dr. Sloan's words, but I still can't stop thinking of what could have happened if he had not moved the Bigfoot out of the room. I try to calm myself and remain professional.

Question

May I please have a glass of water… and directions to the men's room?

Sloan

Certainly, Mr. Plainview.

We are very fortunate that Dr. Sloan has provided us with an actual excerpt from his own personal journal kept at the BF Eco-Habitat. It may be noted that Dr. Sloan is not legally obligated to provide this information.

-Dr Chandler F. Sloan's Personal Journal Account # 4103

Date: October 27, 20**

Time: 1:18 am

Location: BF Eco-Habitat

Weather: Partial moon, clear night
      41°F

Notes:

* 2 BF Juggernauts pulled into the facility after a mainline communication, security was alerted.

* We were prepped and ready when they arrived.

* The transitioning of the 2 new specimens proved to be moderately difficult, they needed to be separated and sedated.

* My technicians are on extended overtime and are somewhat disgruntled, but they must stay on until lock down is complete per their contract.

* Of the two specimens obtained, one is a very aggressive male and the other is a female. Male approx 7ft 8 in., Female approx 6ft 9 in.

* From information gathered from the Juggernaut technicians, the male specimen seems to have been entangled in a salmon fishing net on the edge of the Rogue River.

* The Juggernaut techs said the female could have escaped at any time, but she chose not to leave the male... very interesting

* Note: Loading area must get better illumination/area is too dark to work in, uncomfortable/dangerous

* Specimens show what seem to be heavy scratches around neck and shoulders, perhaps induced by mating.

* The male is missing two fingers on the right hand, and has a festering wound on the upper left hip.

* Female is very alert and agitated, but appears to be in sound health.

* BF Crippler had to be used on the male in our first attempt to move him into our holding/decontamination container.

* The female was placed into the container opposite the male.

* Both creatures were given water (with electrolytes) and both refused to drink.

* My technicians went home at 3:04 am, and at lock down time I heard a sad moaning sound from the female's container.

* I will prepare blood and tissue samples first thing in the morning, as well as the normal "new creature procedures" (Micro-Chip and entry, body/limb measurement, complete physicals, dental and eye breakdowns)

* Both specimens will not be introduced into the BF Eco-Habitat until temperament evaluations and health regulations have been met. (Approx 3 weeks)

* Remember to contact Dr. Maddox about the recently obtained creatures, and forward to him all preliminary statistics.

* The male has a tremendous scream / howl, the loudest I have heard so far. (VERY DISTURBING)

Friends of Bigfoot

There is an extreme leftwing group called the "Friends of Bigfoot" (FOB). They claim to be a peaceful group in support of Bigfoot rights and the creature's well being. This group is headed by a man named Terrance Vermeer. He started this grass roots organization in San Francisco in 20**. The group has since blossomed to 37,000 strong. They have held many peaceful protests in Washington, as well as picketed the Langley research facility. The group started as a small band of five people when negative information leaked out from the Bigfoot facility located in the Cascade Mountains. The stories that came out of the facility not only indicated that there were actual Bigfoot in captivity, but that brutal experimentations were being done on these innocent creatures.

In 20**, they plotted to break into the Cascade facility and release whatever Bigfoot were being held there. They planned a huge undertaking which involved a serious financial backer, who never revealed his or her identity to the group. An elaborate scheme was formed in which fictitious positions, titles, and authority clearances were made up and supported by fake identification cards, finger print scans, retinal readouts, and voice recognition composites.

A group of nine people made a daring nighttime break-in. They were not only able to breach the security system, but were able to take down five security guards by use of "stun spray". This was a new government deterrent that was being used to capture Bigfoot, and somehow the group managed to obtain several canisters. FOB were able to release three Bigfoot from captivity. Not one person was hurt as the stun spray is basically an airborne sleeping pill.

After the Bigfoot were released into the wild, the group disbanded and went their separate ways. However, one member of the group remained close to the Cascade facility after the incident, and was apprehended by government officials. He was immediately arrested and brought into an interrogation area and debriefed.

As a result of this break-in and release of the Bigfoot, the subsequent arrest and interrogation of a FOB member and disclosure of what occurred, information leaked onto the internet and the public outcry was massive. The general public was shocked, first of all, that there were captive Bigfoot, and second, they were equally upset that experimentation was being done on the species. The "Friends of Bigfoot "organization has never publicly admitted to this crime.

Dealing with Bigfoot on a Practical Level

BF Crippler

The laws connected with Bigfoot have been increasing because of people pushing the envelope by brutalizing and victimizing the creatures. Due to the large amount of Bigfoot sightings in urban areas, the government has started the "Citizens' Self-Help Program" that describes the use of items that could help ward off a potential Bigfoot attack. Although the Bigfoot has been deemed a mostly docile creature, there are cases where it has been seen as wild and unruly.

The government has since manufactured a BF Crippler which is now available to the public. This is a hand-held taser used as a defense/training tool. It follows all protocol similar to a firearm, such as background checks and a 30 day wait period.

The BF Crippler is an incredibly strong taser gun, and should not be compared to a standard taser. Through the use of modern technology, the BF Crippler's unique design allows the unit to power a large electric channeled pulse up to 20 feet that immobilizes its victim instantly -- in this case, a Bigfoot. This tool which was designed by the military has the strength to kill the average man, so extreme caution must be used.

This powerful tool is mainly used for defense, containment, modifying behavior, and teaching. It is a public security item for the common everyday man. The BF Crippler comes with a training manual, a special 220 "amp-up" recharging adapter, and a holster made of unique branded leather that is worn on the hip. The BF Crippler comes standard with any legitimate license to own a Bigfoot.

BF Juggernaut

These vehicles of semi-futuristic military-design are used to capture wild, rogue or out-of-control creatures and are well-equipped to move through mountainous and heavily forested areas as well as urban surroundings.

There are twenty-eight BF Juggernauts in existence at the moment and all come with the following standard components:
- 2 ½ inch carbon riveted steel throughout the entire vehicle
- Shatterproof UV honed windshield glass (covered with wide titanium steel rods)
- Extreme multilevel illumination in all directions
- An onboard A1 Stratus computer system with microchip detection
- GPS tracking

Military high-tech equipment includes:
- Eight side by side and .44 gauge track guns
- Cobalt phosphorus flairs
- Aastor Net propelling system
- Capacity for knockout gas sweeping
- BF Cripplers
- BF Stun spray
- Several high caliber firearms including a dual barrel rail gun and thermal-pulse rifles
- Night vision capabilities

The vehicle, standing at an impressive 16 feet high and 32 feet long, can transport two captive or wild 800 pound beasts at a time. Ruggedly ominous and a military technological marvel, the BF Juggernaut is truly a non-stoppable force. The BF Juggernaut comes in only one exterior color, flat black, with a periwinkle blue interior.

BF Crippler

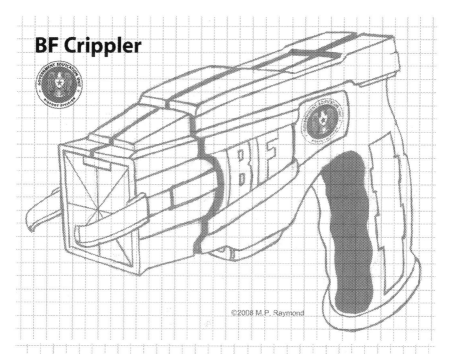

©2008 M.P. Raymond

BF Juggernaut

©2008 M.P. Raymond

Containment Check Stations

We have twenty containment check stations located in remote areas strategically placed throughout the country. These sites, designed by the military, are temporary holding facilities that are well equipped with trained professionals, BF Cripplers, and 24 hour security. There is a toll-free number that can be accessed 24/7 through your local authorities, to be used when a Bigfoot is encountered in an area that would be considered sensitive. When a situation occurs a BF Juggernaut will be sent out into the area to handle the conflict. The Bigfoot will be removed from the area and will be brought to the nearest containment check station. The creature will be held here for a period of time before being shipped to a government facility for a more thorough evaluation.

The majority of check stations are located in the Northwestern area of the country, as this is where the greatest concentration of these creatures exists.

To educate the public concerning the call center process, we have included a segment from the BF Stations report log.

Listed below are just a few examples from the Bigfoot Call Center System. You can observe each situation and the action needed to ensure security for life and property.

BF Call Station Report Log

Monday, September 21, 2:09 a.m. Montana – A middle-aged man is exfoliating his lower back when he hears a sound outside his mobile home. He investigates and discovers a Bigfoot peering into his living room window.

*   Action taken: A BF Juggernaut was dispatched to the location. Unfortunately, the Bigfoot had retreated back

into the surrounding wooded area before field technicians arrived.

Thursday, September 24, 10:14 a.m. California – A large male Bigfoot is seen frantically digging in a small landslide, throwing rocks, while apparently searching for something.

* Action taken: A BF Juggernaut arrives, and field crew technicians use a BF Crippler to immobilize the creature and move it to the nearest check station. Later a female Bigfoot was discovered in the landslide rubble.

Friday, October 2, 1:29 a.m. Oregon – A young boy wakes from a bad dream and spots a Bigfoot from his bedroom window. The creature is observed walking into the family's open garage.

* Action taken: When the BF Juggernaut arrives the Bigfoot becomes extremely agitated. A BF Crippler is used while the creature tries to flee the area. Field technicians pronounced the Bigfoot, dead on arrival at the nearest check station.

Saturday, October 3, 3:42 p.m. Washington – An old woman is sitting on her front porch cleaning one of her collectable throwing knives. She suddenly notices a Bigfoot coming out of the tree line onto her property, and moving directly toward her. She panics and runs inside to call the authorities. While on the phone, the creature walks along her porch and is seen peering into the windows.

* Action taken: A BF Juggernaut arrives. The creature kept a wide distance from the technicians therefore rendering the BF Crippler useless. Net propelling system was deployed. The creature was moved to the nearest check station.

Religion

The religious sector has been very concerned about these Bigfoot discoveries and its placement in the evolutionary scale. Its existence has caused a lot of disruptions to certain religious views and there have been heated discussions at the Vatican and other religious circles all across the country and the world. This has shaken the foundation of many faiths!

Is Bigfoot our descendant, or is it from a different branch of the tree of life that did not continue to evolve with today's modern man?

It is not the goal of this text to solidify any position that the Bigfoot creature is in any way connected to our evolutionary line. However, it is quite apparent that the creature does in fact resemble man in its gait, posture, and facial features/expressions, more so than any other known primate.

Be that as it may, many upper-echelon religious figures, including a certain cardinal at the Vatican, have been at the helm of a group pushing forward to minimize any Bigfoot study. The cardinal has been very active in the internal workings of the Vatican in Rome, presenting lectures on exactly why Bigfoot is considered just another animal. This cardinal's view on Bigfoot seems to be more focused on the implication of what this could possibly mean on a religious level. He has been rallying politicians to stand by him and support him and his cause. The Vatican stands behind this particular cardinal, but itself remains quiet on the issue.

Laws

No citizen will be allowed to capture or house a Bigfoot without a government-issued license. The license issued to use a Bigfoot for farm work, labor in fields, and processing plants is subject to extremely tight supervision. The supervision is carried out by government officials who have been trained to work closely with Bigfoot. There is an incredibly large fine and imprisonment if you do not have a license and you are caught with a Bigfoot in your possession.

Another law states that it is illegal to own Bigfoot hide, teeth, fingernails, or anything biological in nature. This also applies to substances such as blood, saliva, urine, feces, or anything that could be broken down and tested and evaluated. These items cannot be on your person, in your home, in your car, or at your place of work. Being caught with these materials is considered a felony and will lead to prosecution.

Bigfoot falls into the category of an extremely endangered species. From the latest census figures, there are only 972 documented creatures today in this country. It is the responsibility of the government to diligently protect this species in any way possible.

Licensure

The possession of the Bigfoot is not always considered illegal. With the proper licenses and facilities one can own and control this large creature. The status symbols of yesterday no longer exist; the pleasure yachts, the BMWs, the personal jets are now passé. In today's world the ultimate status symbol is to own your own Bigfoot. There are different levels of licensure that shall be granted to qualifying individuals under the proper conditions.

To obtain a first level license, the following conditions must be met:
1. The Bigfoot's microchip information must be logged with the proper government database.
2. The home outside dwelling must be large enough and secure enough to accommodate the large creature.
3. The government can at any time enter the property to check on the status of the animal.

4. Without notice, the government can come and reclaim the creature for research and study.

To obtain a second level license to use the creature strictly for work purposes, the requirements are much more extensive and detailed.

To obtain a third level license to use the Bigfoot creature for security purposes involves even more special requirements than the second level license.

Those who are fortunate enough to be among the select few to be granted a Bigfoot license, one must bear in mind that this is not only a privilege, but a weighty responsibility. All levels of Bigfoot license holders will be expected to follow all rules, regulations, and protocols that have been outlined.

As one might imagine, there are many Bigfoot ownership regulations connected with security, facility/living quarters, and the public safety. These regulations are extremely precise and detailed and will not be discussed in this manual, nor should they be. They are for the license holder's eyes only -- for those who have already passed the stringent requirements necessary to even be considered a potential license holder and then pass all government inspections and examinations in order to have the license bestowed on them.

Upon being approved for the license, a separate briefing and edification session will commence. A separate highly classified manual will be issued at that session. That manual will contain all regulations and protocols that must be followed without question by all Bigfoot license holders. The pains and penalties that will be incurred if these rules are not followed will be serious and severe.

There is an official "Pros and Cons" list (shown below) derived from reports of households that have a working Bigfoot on their property or farm. These civilian locations are part of an ongoing and intensive study program. The government has access to these locations 24 hours a day, seven days a week, and at no time will they need to provide a notice for a random visitation, update, or site evaluation.

Each individual Bigfoot that is placed at any of these designated farm facilities has been intensely screened, trained, and matched according to the creature's personality, farm's needs (if applicable), property, regional layout, and total compliance of the property owner.

Pros
- Security
- Heavy lifting (timber, rocks, engine blocks... basically a hairy fork truck)
- Hearing/eyesight (better than a watchdog)
- No labor unions to contend with
- Status symbol
- Impervious to weather
- Waste (excellent fertilizer)
- Neighborhood intimidation tool
- Participation in on-going government studies

Cons
- Huge food expenses (fruit, fish, mice, greens)
- Moody temperament
- Harassment by environmentalists
- Stench
- Cost of BF taxes, BF licenses, BF vaccinations, BF insurance
- Large sleep shed has to be built
- Constant fence repairs due to frequent escape attempts (containment maintenance)
- Doesn't work well with other animals (cows, horses, dogs, llamas)
- Works only at night and never during a full moon

Things to Be Considered In the Home

If a licensed and trained Bigfoot is on your property, it must always be housed outdoors in a secured area. If the need arises for the creature to enter the home dwelling, there are some things to be considered.

Taking pictures with a camera has proved to be very upsetting to a Bigfoot. Raising the camera to its eye level makes it nervous and agitated. It sees the camera as akin to a firearm. The end result could be that people would get hurt. Refrain from taking photographs or video of a Bigfoot.

Keep Bigfoot out of the bathroom, as it is fascinated with the faucets, running water, and mirrors. These items will make the creature become obsessed and difficult to control. Have a BF Crippler charged and ready at all times.

Ceiling fans are another problem for a Bigfoot, and for obvious reasons. These should be removed from the premises or be in an area not accessible to the Bigfoot.

Radios, TVs, iPods, or anything small and electrical are said to be a distraction or a hindrance for a Bigfoot. These items tend to soothe, almost mesmerize Bigfoot. They can also cause problems when trying to train the creature. These items should be removed in order to have better training results. Also remember, no one can be eating or smoking when a Bigfoot is in the home.

Bigfoot-Proofing your Home and Property

- A great deterrent to Bigfoot is the installation of an 18-foot high heavy gauge chain-linked fence around the property, topped with razor wire. This has proven to be most effective in keeping Bigfoot from harassing the average citizen.

- Motion detecting sensors located at the outside corners of the home and in front of doors and windows is another effective protection device.
- A great idea is to acquire the special Bigfoot-proof garbage cans which are now available. These heavy duty canisters will block out food odors and have a special dial locking system to prevent any Bigfoot gaining entrance.
- Keep all canines and cats indoors at night.
- Chickens, sheep, pigs and any other livestock should be kept inside a fenced enclosure.
- Have direct phone access to your local BF Juggernaut dispatch unit in case of encountering an aggressive Bigfoot.

Dealing with an Aggressive Bigfoot

- Immediately drop to the ground, curl into a ball and begin humming. This disorients the creature and confuses it. Humming a series of low tones has a soothing effect on the agitated Bigfoot. Stay in this curled position until the Bigfoot loses interest and moves on.
- After it leaves the area, seek a secure location.
- Contact authorities (BF Juggernaut dispatch unit) immediately.

Other Potential Problems

There are other problems for the everyday man who owns a Bigfoot for use on his farm or in his barn, or in his home. Waste or fecal removal is one item of note. The Bigfoot can in fact be trained not to defecate in the home zone. This typically takes time, as Bigfoot will usually just "go" when the urge hits it.

In the home, Bigfoot cannot sit at the kitchen or dining room table. It is just too big and its odor is just too offensive. It needs to eat outdoors. For the Bigfoot creature, and also for its owner, time and patience are the keys to success.

Studies have shown that Bigfoot enjoys being sprayed down by a hose. Trying to bathe a Bigfoot in any kind of receptacle such as a large tub or pool has not been successful. Pond or lake bathing seems to be the best and most ideal approach for the creature.

There is a large learning curve, much of which the government is just starting to realize and understand. The obtaining of new data is making the transition to living with Bigfoot in a family setting practical and realistic.

Dealing with the Bigfoot Smell

Bigfoot has very delicate skin under its hair. It possesses a lot of oil glands and it secretes a very musty, pungent, obnoxious odor. At no time should anyone try to mask or eliminate this scent from the Bigfoot. It has been proven in tests at the Cascade facility that every time this was attempted the results have been negative. A wide variety of home remedies have been tested, such as tomato juice, scented aloe, and various other natural ingredients. Nothing seems to work, and it seems that the Bigfoot will break out in a very bad rash under its hair.

There was also an attempt to use gasoline, which has detergent properties, and the results were horrible. At this point while studying and trying to understand them, it appears that we should not interfere with their natural scent. In the Langley facility trials are underway with a new product that will neutralize the scent for humans, but will not mask it for other Bigfoot. Until this product is perfected and introduced, we will have to deal with their odorous scent.

Illegal Body Part Usage

There are many parts of the Bigfoot body that have rumored

to be helpful and useful for a variety of conditions. These are all considered illegal activities by the government, and anyone caught or suspected of use will be prosecuted.

- Bigfoot (Palmbulbus) glands are highly odorous and are located in the hide, along the spinal column, and in the hind region. The secretions can be used to make a topical ointment that has been shown to be an excellent deterrent from mosquitoes and when mixed with egg yolk has impressive adhesive properties.
- Bigfoot hair has been tested and shown to exhibit great insulating properties. Scientists have used DNA gene signatures to recreate and synthesize a version that uses fifty percent less material and still increases thermals by one hundred percent. These studies have been conducted by our government, and are considered legal, but it must be stated that anyone who is found in possession of a hide or any amount of hair will be prosecuted.
- Bigfoot tooth enamel that is ground down to a powder extract and combined with hot tea has been shown to generate an aphrodisiacal sensation. This compound has become so popular that it sells for over $100,000 a gram. It seems a lot of teeth have been stolen from the original Bigfoot burial site in Ape Canyon. This site was thought to be a secure location and yet it was later discovered to have been raided over a period of five weeks of skulls, hands, and of course, teeth.
- Another illegal usage of Bigfoot parts has been conducted by the Chinese. They boil down Bigfoot fat and make a highly nutritious soup that is said to give the one who eats it incredible vitality.

Other illegal activity connected with Bigfoot have also recently surfaced, such as black-market trading, moving Bigfoot creatures between dwellings that have not been microchipped, training the creatures in specific ways that have not been government approved, such as non-regulated and undocumented breeding.

Hunting this creature is also strictly forbidden. Any intention of trying to cause a Bigfoot any harm comes directly with a stiff fine and mandatory imprisonment. Large hunting parties in the Klamath Mountain Range have been arrested, as well as lone weekend hunters. This behavior will absolutely not be tolerated on any level.

Capitalization of Bigfoot

In recent years the idea of using the Bigfoot name, image, or persona as a means of marketing has grown by leaps and bounds beyond what anyone could ever have imagined. The greater the amount of publicity that has been given to Bigfoot, the more notorious its name and image have become. It has become commonplace for Bigfoot's representation, likeness, name, size, and stature to be found on a great number of commercially available items.

The numerous Bigfoot-related objects range from simple to complex: Bigfoot toilet paper, toothbrushes, Bigfoot cereal, shoes, sneakers, various footwear, the new Bigfoot SUV, the new Bigfoot line of clothing created to be the fashionable new rugged wear of today, a Bigfoot travel bag for the person that needs to pack everything for that short trip, Bigfoot camping gear, a number of newly-built schools in the Northwest (having names such as Sasquatch Academy of Science and Technology, The Bigfoot Institute of Learning), a new sitcom about "Big Boy" the Bigfoot who is befriended by a local Cascade mountain family, and even a series of movies that depict Bigfoot as a savior of the earth, fighting against invading aliens.

Big-Food is a new fast food chain stating up in the Midwest that is gaining a great deal of popularity. The chain features extra large burgers, fries, and shakes. They also offer Sasquatch kids' portions. The Big-Food mascot is a large Sasquatch named "Big Saq", shown on television commercials wearing a red & white checked chef's hat and apron. This is only a sample of how the Bigfoot name and image have been exploited by anyone who has a desire to make money off the giant creature.

Zoo/Photographic Safari Tours

A major zoo in upstate California has just purchased five Bigfoot to become a permanent addition to their facility. Construction of a new Bigfoot World will be completed within two years, at a cost of 72 million dollars. A waiting list has already been established for the premiere opening.

Photographic safari tours are becoming a new sensation as well; they consist of a guided excursion into several known Bigfoot locations along the Klamath Mountains. This is a seven-day excursion, complete with lodging and food. The paying customers will be visiting several of the Bigfoot hotspots. Safaris are now being booked seven months in advance.

CHECKLIST

- Things Bigfoot likes to eat in the wild
    - o Fermented choke cherries
    - o Salmon (high protein intake)
    - o Trout
    - o Wild mushrooms
    - o Wood Grubs
    - o Mice
    - o Dandelion greens
    - o Blueberries
    - o Wild onions

- Things Bigfoot likes to eat in captivity
    - o Hawaiian pizza
    - o Sweet potatoes
    - o Extra-crunchy peanut butter
    - o Hard-boiled eggs
    - o Gelatin (lime)
    - o Biscotti
    - o Beef jerky
    - o Cheese popcorn
    - o Tuna fish sandwiches
    - o Limes
    - o Sardines

- Things not to feed Bigfoot in captivity
    - o Cantaloupe
    - o String Cheese
    - o Salsa (hot)
    - o Milk Chocolate
    - o Alfredo sauce
    - o Avocado

- o Funnel cake
- o Bubble gum
- o Hard candy
- o Black licorice
- o Szechuan food (not ever!)
- o Soda (especially ginger ale)

- Things not to do with Bigfoot
  - o Sneak up on it
  - o Shout at it
  - o Carry a firearm or camera
  - o Look at it directly in the eye (challenges it)
  - o Show extreme emotion (anger, fear, crying)
  - o Wrestle with it

- Things Bigfoot likes
  - o Humming/whispering voices (soothes it)
  - o Singing
  - o Having its hands or forearms rubbed
  - o River bathing/running water
  - o Rubbing back against trees
  - o Physical contact (with its own kind)
  - o Television/radio

- Bigfoot play items
  - o Beach balls/balloons
  - o Heavy rope with a large knot on the end
  - o Tractor tires
  - o Bells
  - o Garden hose (running water)

- Things not to let Bigfoot have
  - o Adhesive tape
  - o Hammers
  - o Golf balls

- o Mirrors
- o Chalking guns

- Signs of Bigfoot agitation
    - o Twisting small tree tops
    - o Rock throwing
    - o Stomping/howling/grimacing
    - o Swaying/pacing back and forth

The rediscovery of Bigfoot is not unlike that of other species that were thought to be extinct, but for reasons beyond us all, are actually thriving. Consider the stories of the Chacoan Peccary, Coelacanth, and the height-sensitive Red Crested Button Bird. All of these creatures were thought to be extinct, passed on years ago, but in actuality were living in isolated regions of the world. As man has encroached on these small parts of the world and has spread his tentacles in search of land, food, natural resources, and power, these innocent creatures are subject to losing the sensitive environment that has kept them so perfectly cloaked in secrecy. Once they are found, the delicate balance they once had is lost; and man, who disturbed their world, must now step in and help to protect them. For every man who wants to help and protect these groups, there are ten who will want to exploit them.

The information you have just received in this text includes all that the government is willing to release on the subject at this time. Officially, we strongly urge the country to refer to this text, follow its direction, and to recognize the importance of the Bigfoot Civilian Edification Form. When a point is reached where more relevant information is declassified, a modified manual will be released.

Conclusion

The sun is setting outside my office window and it has put me in a reflective state. The writing of this manual has made me think in a slightly different direction than when I started. On a personal level for me this text has stirred up more questions than answers. I wonder who we are as human beings and what we feel we're entitled to.

Too many species in our lifetime have become endangered and even extinct. This country's views and our public value system will dictate how this manual will be received. We have set forth up-to-date, precise, and relevant information with the intent of providing a sense of security and awareness. We realize that this information is difficult for some individuals to comprehend, but trust in your government to lead you through.

Bigfoot is unique and not like any other animal, and therefore our perception and respect for it should reflect that. This creature of myth and legend has now become a part of our culture. To truly understand Bigfoot, maybe we can obtain a better understanding of ourselves. In your daily existence you should continue on and proceed with your lives and remember -- we are protecting, securing, and watching all. On behalf of the government, I would like to thank you for your attention concerning this sensitive topic.

Stuart Plainview – Government Liaison

MANDATORY BIGFOOT CIVILIAN EDIFICATION FORM

I _____ on this date: _____ 20____

state that I have thoroughly read the Government manual entitled "Bigfoot Declassified" and I hereby vow to follow all said rules and regulations, parameters, guidelines, and instructions of said manual set forth by the government. Upon signing and dating the said document, it will be returned to the government process center for logging into the National Bigfoot Master Reference listing. I understand that by not signing and returning this document to the government, that I will be opening myself up to intimidation, fines and possible imprisonment. Also, by not submitting to this Government issue I surrender any rights otherwise given to me for protection from legal manifestations listed under Article #10-20-1967RPRG.

Signature: _____

Witness: _____

Witness to your Witness: _____

Date: _____

Mail Form (in an opaque security envelope) back to:
  Bigfoot Civilian Edification Form
  PO Box 10201967
  Washington. DC 100100

ACKNOWLEDGMENTS

Many heartfelt thanks go out to Jim Kempskie for his patience with this project, Alison Lee for her wonderful design abilities, my beautiful daughter Lindsey Marie for her love and support, and Mark Comeau for the gift of his great friendship.

A huge acknowledgement goes out to a few of the Bigfoot investigation leaders themselves: John Green, Rene Dahinden, Rick Noll, Daniel Perez, John Bindernagel, Jeff Meldrum, Dmitri Bayanov, Peter Byrne, Bob Titmus, Loren Coleman and Ivan Sanderson.

Very special thanks goes out to the late Grover Krantz for his courage, perseverance and being a true man of science who understood that a true scientist is one that delves into the unknown.

And of course -- Roger Patterson and Bob Gimlin for creating the film footage that left such a huge impression on a 9-year-old boy.

Thank you so much!!

MPR